Laurie Yost's middle n
fine with that. As a v
allows Jesus to take
mistakes, erupting em~......
them to show her transparency and sincerity to reach women
of all walks of life. Each chapter is drenched in humor and love,
guaranteeing that every woman can relate to her testimony!
Enjoy and be blessed!

Cyndy Gusler
Author and Speaker - From The Vine Ministries
www.FromTheVineMinistries.com

Laurie has blessed me with her friendship for some fifteen
years. She is a dynamic speaker and writer. I've had the unique
privilege to be in both her speaking and writing audiences.
From my seat, she's hilarious, engaging, inspiring and Jesus-
filled when sharing her ministry and her heart.

Melanie Pickett
Writes at melaniespickett.com and defyingshadows.com
Has been featured in Whole Magazine, Splickety Magazine,
BlogHer, and Breathe Writers Conference blog

Not only does Laurie present her life situations in a funny, "I
can't believe that really happened" way, she also is quick to
share how God works through her. I think you will enjoy owning
your own copy of this book and also being able to dig deeper
into God's Word.

Kris Klassen
Former WMI President East MI Conference of the Free
Methodist Church

I don't know how so many mishaps happen to one person, but Laurie has a gifted way of sharing personal stories that will make you laugh so hard you cry (and be thankful that it didn't happen to you). Laurie encourages you to laugh and sit at Jesus' feet and learn from Him. I highly recommend Laurie as a speaker and author. You will not be disappointed!

Rev. Joy Ziegler, Senior Pastor of 37 North Wesleyan Church Southgate, Michigan
http://www.joy-ziegler.blogspot.com

Stumbling Along

*One Woman's Journey of Falling into Embarrassing
and Hilarious Moments.*

Laurie Yost

WESTBOW
P R E S S*
A DIVISION OF THOMAS NELSON
& ZONDERVAN

WestBow Press books may be ordered through booksellers or by contacting:

WestBow Press
A Division of Thomas Nelson & Zondervan
1663 Liberty Drive
Bloomington, IN 47403
www.westbowpress.com
1 (866) 928-1240

ISBN: 978-1-5127-1602-3 (sc)
ISBN: 978-1-5127-1603-0 (hc)
ISBN: 978-1-5127-1601-6 (e)

Library of Congress Control Number: 2015916941

Print information available on the last page.

WestBow Press rev. date: 10/23/2015

Contents

Foreword

Laurie Yost makes me laugh out loud at her life. In fact, she made me laugh out loud the first time we met at a comedy show. So her publishing a funny book does not come as a surprise to me. In this humorous, inside look at her life, you will find not only is she funny, but she is open, honest, and really puts herself out there.

I love the comical stories of accidents, embarrassing moments, and just plain being awkward. I can relate to that. We can *all* relate to that. Most of all, I appreciate how Laurie puts an encouraging and inspirational spin on her silly moments in life. This book helps us take a look at our own life and find the funny. Without life, what stories would we have to tell? What if our own life might give hope and laughter to others? Laurie shows us just how to do that.

Fortunately for us, the Bible says laughter is medicine. We all need to laugh just a little bit more. Okay, a lot more. Thank you, Laurie, for putting yourself out there so we can laugh at

you...I mean laugh with you. You are funny and inspirational.
I think now I'll go laugh at myself.

Donna East
Comedian

Acknowledgments

This book was born from years of stories and adventures going back to my childhood. I would first like to thank my mom, Sharon, for giving birth to me after thirty-six long, painstaking hours, only for me to come out breech (legs first). This world entry started my journey of incidents and accidents and knowing quickly that I wasn't going to do things the *normal* way. I'd like to thank both of my parents, Jim and Sharon, for their influence on my life; they have always encouraged me to live my dreams.

I'd like to dedicate this book to my Prince Charming, my wonderful, kind, and patient husband, Brian, who has been by my side for twenty-seven years. Thank you for tending my wounds, laughing at my stumbles, telling me that I should write these silly stories into a book, and always loving me for me. You are a true gift from God. I love you.

Thank you to my children, Mitchell, Zachary, and Emily. You have lived these stories with me. You have shaken your heads in embarrassment and laughed when you couldn't do anything else. You have grown into young men and a woman of the Lord who make me proud. I love watching you do life. You three are amazing.

My sister Beth was a huge help early on with her editorial expertise. She graciously met with me over Skype (while I lived in Mexico and she in California) to pound out the details of organizing the book and to begin the writing process. Thank you for giving me direction.

I'd like to thank Rhonda Riffel, Melanie Pickett, Kris Klassen, Lisa Devine, Eileen Jarvis, Cyndy Gusler, Aisha Hernandez Norzagaray de Torres, Nicki Rockwell, Sylvia Yost, Judy Shinabarger, and Trish Stiles. These are the gals with whom I've bounced off ideas, and asked for grammar help, input, and suggestions. Though they have lives and families of their own, they helped me as they were able. For that I am grateful. Also, thank you to my many blog and Facebook followers who have commented on my stories throughout the years and have motivated me to go forward in writing.

I'm grateful to Brad and Alicia Reinke from Simple Pleasures Photography. They used their creative ideas in taking promo photos and cover shots. Big thanks to my daughter, Emily, who risked tumbling down the stairs posing for the cover photo.

Thank you to Westbow Press for help in making this dream possible. Thank you to Kayla Stobaugh, my check-in coordinator, to Alex and all of the editing staff and to the amazing and creative design staff.

Finally, I would like to thank our Lord Jesus Christ for His faithfulness to me. Through my life's stumbles He has been my refuge and my strength. To serve and follow Him has been my joy and my privilege. Thank You, Lord, for choosing the imperfect me to do Your work.

Part I

It Could Happen to You (but Hopefully It Won't)

Chapter 1

The Awkward Giraffe

When people ask me to describe myself, one of the words that never gets left out is *clumsy*. I usually say that I'm a *little* clumsy, but if I'm totally honest with myself, I have to admit that I am *a lot* clumsy. I'm not sure why, but things just sort of happen to me. I try to be careful, but the cracks in the sidewalk will rise up just as I get to them, a mud puddle will appear as I walk by, and I'll misjudge where a wall is and slam my shoulder into it. How is it possible to be walking with someone through the church and actually trip on the carpet? That is a hard question for me to answer because I truly don't know. But it has happened to me, and more than once!

One of the definitions I found for *clumsy* is one who lacks physical coordination, skill, or grace; someone who is awkward. *Awkward?* This word makes me think of a big, tall giraffe. Funny thing is that in the Philippines and in Mexico, I *am* looked at as a big, tall giraffe (or giant). At five feet, eight, some say I am a "tall drink of water" for a lady. And my big-boned stature adds to that. For the record, I don't like the term *big-boned* because it makes me feel like someone is just trying to find a nicer way to say "hefty" or "with much girth."

Ah, but the word *grace* or *graceful*. Now this is a word that makes me think of someone who flutters about with ease, who tears up the dance floor with just her presence, and who can do several things at a time with, what seems like, little effort. Some would say the older and more mature you get the more graceful you become. I'm forty-seven years old and still looking forward to that. Maybe the magic number is fifty.

As a pastor's wife and missionary, there are times I have had to be up front, where the focus is on me. These are the times I desire to be a little more graceful than others. I recall several years ago, after traveling ten hours on a bumpy dirt road in the Philippines, we arrived at our destination and were ushered to the front table to have dinner before giving our workshops. We were extremely tired after so many hours of travel, but it was one of those moments when we just couldn't lay our heads down on the table and go to sleep. We were the guests of honor and needed to act with a bit of poise. I was wearing a cream-colored outfit because it traveled well and was appropriate for speaking in front of an audience. In the midst of my fatigue, I was trying really hard to be professional as people watched us, their guests, eat.

The people were thrilled to have us in their city, and they had made a wonderful meal of a type of meat, gravy, and potatoes mixed together, with white rice on the side. As I began to enjoy my meal, I took the next bite, bumped the plate with my elbow, and dumped its entire contents down the front of me. How is it possible for these things to happen to me in moments like this? I'm supposed to have some grace and poise—not be a clumsy oaf.

You have to wonder what the people we had just met thought of this clumsy American lady. There was nothing else to do but spoon the food from my clothes back onto my plate. Of course, the ladies who were serving wanted to give me another plate, which, in turn, drew more attention to my lack of grace. Several thin napkins later and an evident stain on my cream-colored outfit, I went on with the evening, finished my next plate with no spills, spoke up front, and returned to my room to soak my clothes in cold water.

My *graceful* evening ended with me lying in my bed, watching the ants make their paths across the ceiling, doing their work with their own bit of grace. I wondered how God could ever use this awkward giraffe (me) for His glory.

The funny thing about my short trip to the Philippines to minister to others was the comment one pastor's wife made to me. She said, "Laurie, you are so tall and beautiful, and your nose is so beautiful as well. Here we are so short, and our noses are so flat and small." Recalling the many times of being teased about my height, and especially my nose while growing up, I told her that, with daily comments like that, I might just move there and live with her.

You see, being tall, clumsy, and a little awkward is okay. It's all perspective. I have the privilege of helping little old ladies get things off the top shelves in the grocery store and encouraging them with a smile. My height can be a good conversation starter for people who can't believe any woman could be so tall. My lack of grace can be an icebreaker in a stuffy situation. God has used all of this for His glory.

I was reading recently Psalm 139 (NIV) where it says, "You are fearfully and wonderfully made." It also says in the same chapter, "God saw my unformed body before it came to be." He knew me. He knows me. He loves me. That wonderfully made part includes my height and my big nose. This awkward giraffe is totally, 100 percent loved by God!

Digging Deeper

1. It seems the world today is always telling us and showing us through media and magazines that we have to look the *perfect* way. To you, what truly is the perfect look?

2. What parts of your body do you like the best? What parts of your body do you like the least? Why?

3. Let's look at how God sees you. What words stand out to you in Psalm 139 (NIV) as you read this? Underline them.

   For you created my inmost being;
   you knit me together in my mother's womb.
   I praise you because I am fearfully and wonderfully made;
   your works are wonderful,
   I know that full well.
   My frame was not hidden from you
   when I was made in the secret place,

when I was woven together in the depths of the earth.
Your eyes saw my unformed body;
all the days ordained for me were written in your
book
before one of them came to be.

4. God tells us His works are wonderful. You are one of His works. You are wonderful. In Greek, the word *wonderful* is *thauma*, which means "wondrous, a miracle, a wonderful thing, remarkable, admirable." How does this make you feel?

5. How can you daily look at yourself in the wondrous way God sees you and less how the media tells you to look?

Chapter 2

Almost Sliced by Good Intentions

There is nothing I like more about living in Mexico than meeting new people and visiting with them. I love trying to build relationships and make conversations with others by using what I like to call "Laurie's Spanish." The key word would surely be "trying," because at times, my limited knowledge of the Spanish language keeps me from truly being able to get my point across. Looking back at the many times I have spoken to people, I have to be honest and say that my words have maybe even been a little dangerous.

One May afternoon in 2005, about a year before we were assigned as full-time missionaries to Mexico, I was visiting a friend in her home on the southern Arizona border. We went to a small house across the border into Mexico to do a Bible study. Thankfully, my friend spoke in fluent, wonderful-sounding Spanish, while my Spanish was just what I had learned in high school.

The family invited us into their home so that we could share more about Jesus with them. I was excited to be there. I sat down next to the grandmother and a little girl who was about three years old. Here's a language tip: when you don't know a language very well, little kids are the ones who are the most forgiving. I focused my attention on visiting with the little girl because I thought I wouldn't have to say much; smiling and laughing with her would keep her busy.

This sweet little girl was holding a cute stuffed bunny rabbit. I thought this might be a safe conversation point, where I could insert a few of the Spanish words I knew. I began to make faces at her and her stuffed rabbit and to pet the rabbit. I gently took the rabbit from her, hugged it tightly, and said, "I love your *cuchillo*. I love your cuchillo so much. Let's hug and pet and love on your cuchillo."

As I was speaking, I could see the grandmother out of the corner of my eye looking strangely at me. This look was really nothing new to me, whether in the United States or another country, so I proceeded to make a big deal about this little girl's cuchillo and how lucky she was to have it to hug and love. The little girl enjoyed my antics, and because she did, I just kept going with and overdramatizing them.

When the grandmother could take it no longer, she pointed to the kitchen and for the little girl to go there. She said something to her that I didn't understand, so I just smiled. A few seconds later, this sweet little three-year-old girl came staggering in toward her grandma with a butcher knife. Yes, a *butcher knife*. I started to wonder what in the world was going on in this place and why this little girl was holding on to a butcher knife. When she finally got back to us (thankfully, without stabbing anyone), the grandma looked at me. She pointed to the butcher knife and said "cuchillo" and then pointed at the bunny rabbit and said *"conejo."* Oh, I was using the wrong word for bunny rabbit.

I then began to think about how I must have sounded to the grandmother and the little girl (who was probably still learning words herself). *Let's hug and love your butcher knife. Aren't you so glad that you have a butcher knife to play with? Let's love on your butcher knife with everything in us.*

I learned a lesson that day. I learned how to say bunny rabbit in Spanish. I will have that word carved into my mind forever. I will also have the picture of a toddler, holding a big knife, staggering to her grandmother.

About a year after this experience, we were living in Mexico full time. One would think that I would never forget the word in Spanish for bunny rabbit (conejo), but that wasn't the case. My sister-in-law, Kristy, was visiting our new home in Mexico. I was so excited to introduce her to my friends at the kids' school. Each day, I went to the school to pick them up, so I took her with me one day. When we were allowed to enter the gates to get them (security is very high at the schools), we were standing in the courtyard, waiting for classes to be released. I recognized a few people who walked by, and I said *hola*. Finally, all three of my kids had gathered around, very happy to see Aunt Kristy.

Of course, when we would come to the school, people would take note because we were the only Americans who attended. On this particular day, there was a new American, and so a few of the teachers and the administrator stood around with us. I was very pleased to introduce Kristy to everyone. With a confidence in my voice and proudness in my heart to have a relative with me, I said in my very best Spanish, "I would like to introduce you to my conejo, Kristy."

Any time you introduce someone and there is a pause and strange looks, it's pretty clear something was not said correctly. Finally, my friend, Martina (the kids' very kind and helpful English teacher), told me I had just introduced them to my bunny rabbit, Kristy. I was horrified, as I wanted to present to the school a sense of intelligence on my part. (Fat chance of it happening after *that* remark.) Everyone chuckled, and poor Kristy, having no idea what was going on, just pleasantly said "hola." I just wanted to hide in a hole right there, in the clay dirt of the desert. It was then I learned the word for sister-in-law. It's not what I said, obviously. You would think after my afternoon lesson with bunny rabbit and butcher knife that I would have at least not chosen *that* word. If you ever need to know the word for sister-in-law, it's *cuñada*, not conejo.

It's funny that I said all of those words with such confidence, but I still had them wrong. It didn't matter if I said them louder or with more feeling; they were just plain wrong. Had I studied Spanish vocabulary more, I would have known this. Had I listened to the two years of Spanish I took in high school, I may have saved myself some trouble.

I think we can do the same thing in our lives when it has to do with God. We can know a few of the right *Christian* things to say, and we say them with confidence. But that doesn't really make us a Christ follower, just like my knowing a few Spanish words didn't make me a Spanish speaker. I want to encourage you to begin to have a relationship with

God and know His Word fully so that you can know the way you're living is the right way.

Digging Deeper

1. Read Colossians 4:2–6 (NIV); write down what you read about opportunities. "Devote yourselves to prayer, being watchful and thankful. And pray for us, too, that God may open a door for our message, so that we may proclaim the mystery of Christ, for which I am in chains. Pray that I may proclaim it clearly, as I should. Be wise in the way you act toward outsiders; make the most of every opportunity. Let your conversation be always full of grace, seasoned with salt, so that you may know how to answer everyone."

2. How can we make the most of every opportunity each day?

3. Sometimes we go into situations with such good intentions, as in the case in the story above, and something doesn't go quite right.

    a. Do you think God still can still use those situations to point people toward Himself?
    b. Though I fumbled the language, how might the people in the house I visited have seen Jesus in me?
    c. How have people seen Jesus in you today?

4. Sometimes the thought of helping others gets to be overwhelming. Instead of looking for opportunities to change the whole world, look for opportunities to make a difference right here and right now—where God has placed you.

Chapter 3

Just Bring Yogurt

We moved to the mission field in Mexico in 2006 before we had any language training. (The two years of Spanish in high school didn't count, because I didn't listen as well as I apparently should have.) The idea was for us to find a place along the border to do our schooling. That way we would still be able to live near a few of our strongest churches in Mexico in order to learn how they minister, while learning the language and culture.

It was decided, about a year and a half into this process, that because of the lack of good Spanish schools where we were living, we needed to leave the country to do full-time language studies. Though our Spanish-speaking abilities were minimal, we had learned some while living in the border town. We had met and had begun to build relationships with some wonderful people—all Spanish speakers.

One Sunday we visited a church where we had previously spent a lot of time. I was talking there with a good friend named Lucy. Of course, we weren't talking *during* the church service; it was afterward, when she invited me to the ladies' brunch the following Saturday. I answered, "Yes! I would love to come. What can I bring?"

Lucy replied, "You can bring yogurth, if you want." My mind was spinning. Yogurth, yogurth? Ohhhh, yogurt. I asked, "Where is the brunch going to be?"

"It will be at the fancy restaurant on the top of the hill going out of town," she responded. That was good for me because, in that large city, I actually knew the location.

At this point in my Spanish learning process, it was very important for me to listen well and then repeat back to the person what I understood he or she had just told me. I was implementing a simple Communications 101 course (and my speech teacher would have been very proud of me). I was excited to realize, during this whole exchange, that I had understood everything Lucy had said to me. This was a big deal, and I felt like jumping up and down (I did, however, contain myself). Just to make sure, I repeated it all back to her. "So there is a ladies brunch this next Saturday?"

"Si."

"The brunch starts at 10:00 a.m. at the hotel on the top of the hill?"

"Si."

"You want me to bring yogurt?"

"Si."

I had covered it and was feeling great. Now I knew that I probably wouldn't understand everything that was going to be said at the brunch, but I would be able to understand a few words and get basic ideas. If anything, I knew it would be about God. It's always good to have a starting point—a reference—and that was mine. As we stood there talking, I invited her family to our home for dinner the following Thursday night, and they agreed to come.

The evening of their visit we had a wonderful meal together and sat around the table talking and laughing (mostly them chuckling at us butchering their language and us laughing because we were doing so). I asked Lucy again about the brunch two days later and told her I was excited about coming. I then asked, "So, who do you have coming in to speak? Is she a good speaker? Have you heard her before?"

Lucy got a little grin on her face, as if I must be joking (because we teased each other a lot). She then realized that my question was a serious one, and she answered, "Why, you're the speaker, Laura."

Everything seemed to go in slow motion at that point for me. "*I'm* the speaker?" I responded with wide eyes. At this point, everyone around the table was feeling the awkwardness of the moment as they shifted in their seats and the laughter began. Lucy said, "Yes, Laura. Remember, I asked you on Sunday?"

Oh my, what have I gotten myself into? I silently asked myself. With all of the confidence I could muster I replied, "Of course I remember talking to you on Sunday (I just hadn't remembered the question asked—obviously.) I'll be there and will be more than happy to speak."

We completed our evening together, and the second they walked out the door I started pacing back and forth, questioning what in the world was I going to do. I just stood there in my house, thinking about the fact that, in two days, there were going to be one hundred women expecting from me a twenty-five-minute message in Spanish that I knew I couldn't give.

I started to sweat and fret. Then I realized I was going to have to find a translator and quick. Thankfully, the Lord brought to my mind one of the kids' teachers at the school they attended. Martina had become a good friend of mine, and she was bilingual. She'd been the one who had approached us when we first took the kids to the school and had offered to help us. A true godsend. Now I was going to have to call on her again for help.

I called her that same evening and asked if she was busy Saturday morning. Normally she goes and sells her things at the flea market on Saturday mornings, but for some reason, she was free that particular Saturday. I knew that God had my back on this. He knew, after my conversation with Lucy last Sunday morning that I was going to need Martina. She graciously said she would help me.

On Saturday morning, I walked into the hotel, not only with my yogurt but also with my friend, Martina, at my side. I don't even remember what I spoke about, but I know that I spoke in the best English I could. I spoke with pauses so that Martina could translate for me, and the morning went well. A great blessing was that I was able to introduce Martina to some of my church friends; it later became a way for her to connect with the pastor of this church when her family had a serious problem.

Can you imagine if Lucy and her family had not come over for dinner that Thursday night? Can you picture me walking into the hotel, with my yogurt, greeting everyone and being led to the head table? I just would have thought I was sitting there because I was the missionary. Can you imagine them calling my name to speak and having to get up in front of all those women, with hardly a Spanish word in my mind except *ayudame* (help me)? Thankfully, God knew of the events happening that day, and He put all of those things in place to make sure that He had my back. Instead of the sinking feeling of begging for help when they called my name—not knowing I was supposed to speak—I was able to stand up when they called my name and thank God for the help He had provided me through my wonderful bilingual friend.

Digging Deeper

1. I love the story about Jesus in the boat with the disciples during the big storm. The storm was raging and Jesus was asleep. The disciples grew anxious because it came upon them when they weren't expecting it. Luke 8:24 (NIV) says, "The disciples went and woke him, saying, 'Master, Master, we're going to drown!' He got up and rebuked the wind and the raging waters; the storm subsided, and all was calm."

2. Jesus was the help they needed in a desperate situation. Have you ever called out to Jesus during a desperate time in your life, when you felt like you were drowning? Explain the situation.

3. Jesus was a friend to the disciples. He did what He could to help His friends. He even provides friends for us to help us in times of need, just like he provided Martina for me. Are you the kind of friend who will help someone who is struggling?

4. Ephesians 4:9–10 (NIV) says, "Two are better than one, because they have a good return for their work. If one falls down, his friend can help him up. But pity the man who falls and has no one to help him up!"

5. Thank the Lord today for friends who have helped you out in the past.

Chapter 4

I'm Hot

I don't do well with hot weather. Since I was a kid I have struggled when the sun beats down, and it gets too warm outside. The ironic thing is, as I write this, I am in Mexico during the hottest time of the year, when it gets to be over 110 degrees at times. That's hot! I give thanks for air-conditioning.

In 1999, my husband, Brian, and I led a team to Mexico City on a mission trip. During our previous mission trips to Mexico, the temperature had always been really warm in the summer, and so, naturally, we packed for that type of weather. Little did we realize all of Mexico does not have the same climate. (Imagine that: a huge, long country not all the same temperature.) We would be staying in the mountains outside of Mexico City at a beautiful Bible institute in the midst of the shaded trees, where the temperature never got out of the seventies. At night it got down-right cold. I recall freezing for two nights, and then, on the third night, remembering the souvenir Mexican blanket I had bought to take back to a friend. She ended up being gifted with a gently used blanket, but it had served its purpose for me for a whole week of cool mountainous temperatures.

The interesting thing about this trip was that we didn't spend our days in the mountains, we just slept there. We ministered in other places, where the temperatures were warm during the day like we had expected. We gathered in parks, on basketball courts, in plazas, and in poor neighborhoods. One day, we went to one particular church with the plan of splitting up and going with the members of that church to invite people in the neighborhood to a children's ministry event happening later that evening. It was long before I knew much Spanish, so I was paired up with a young Mexican pastor and two teenaged boys from our own group who knew a bit of Spanish from their high school classes.

We walked quite a bit, and with the afternoon sun blaring down on us, we all began to sweat. We needed some water to keep us from becoming dehydrated. We stopped to rest for a few minutes. As we stopped, I exclaimed in Spanish to this young pastor, "I sure am hot!" I was just trying to make conversation with the little bit of Spanish I knew.

As we began walking again, the teenaged boys with me took me aside, chuckling, and said, "Laurie, do you know what you just told that pastor?"

I was pretty proud of myself for knowing what I'd said and replied, "Of course I do; I said I was hot."

They laughed and jabbed each other in the ribs and said, "You sure did, Laurie; you sure did." I continued walking, finding those two young boys to be rather odd.

It wasn't long before what I had said truly hit me. They had taken their Spanish classes more recently than I had and remembered some of the differences in how we say things in English and how they are translated into Spanish. I realized my phrasing of "I am hot" was a no-no in Spanish, unless you want to tell someone that you want to be with him or her in a sexual way. At that moment, it hit me like a 150-degree heat wave. I didn't know what to say, I didn't know what to do, and I thought I was going to die a slow death right then and there.

I had one goal in mind now; it wasn't to invite these lovely children to the ministry that night, but to try and figure out how to tell this young pastor I had meant to say I was only warm from the sun and nothing else. My goal was quickly halted when I realized I couldn't tell him differently because I didn't know how.

We continued our journey to invite the neighborhood children to our upcoming event. I walked along, with my face red, not from the sun but from the embarrassing words I had used. The boys, well, they just continued to have those adolescent smirks on their faces. We returned to the church to meet up with the group, and I was glad to be in a crowd of other people.

I searched out my husband in the group and took him aside. I had to tell him what horrible thing I had said to this young pastor. I told Brian that I had told that young pastor (casually pointing his way) that I was hot. Brian replied, "Well it is hot." I said, "No, I told him that I was *hot*, you know the *different* kind of hot." Knowing Brian to be a man of wisdom and good solutions to problems, I quickly asked him to tell me what to do about the situation. He laughed, shook his head, and said, "Oh, Laurie, you sure get yourself into messes, don't you? I really don't think there is anything now you can do." So much for the words of wisdom from my pastor-husband that were supposed to be my lifeline.

It's been over ten years since that day, and I honestly don't remember who that young pastor was. We are now serving in Mexico as full-time missionaries, and I have often wondered if I have run into him since we have been in the field. Come to think of it, I do remember a time at a pastor's conference when someone announced our names, and one of the pastors ran out of the auditorium screaming. I don't know; maybe he was just blessed.

Digging Deeper

1. Read James 3:1–9 (NIV). What do you learn about the tongue?

> Not many of you should become teachers, my fellow believers, because you know that we who teach will be judged more strictly. We all stumble in many ways. Anyone who is never at fault in what they say is perfect, able to keep their whole body in check. When we put bits into the mouths of horses to make them obey us, we can turn the whole animal. Or take ships as an example. Although they are so large and are driven by strong winds, they are steered by a very small rudder wherever the pilot wants to go. Likewise,

the tongue is a small part of the body, but it makes great boasts. Consider what a great forest is set on fire by a small spark. The tongue also is a fire, a world of evil among the parts of the body. It corrupts the whole body, sets the whole course of one's life on fire, and is itself set on fire by hell. All kinds of animals, birds, reptiles and sea creatures are being tamed and have been tamed by mankind, but no human being can tame the tongue. It is a restless evil, full of deadly poison. With the tongue we praise our Lord and Father, and with it we curse human beings, who have been made in God's likeness.

2. In the story above I said the wrong word, and it had a totally different meaning than what I expected. We all make those types of mistakes from time to time. But it's the powerful words that continually come from our mouth that may hurt others with which we need to be concerned. Memorize Psalm 19:14 (NLT), and make it the goal of your life as you pursue your relationship with Christ. "May the words of my mouth and the meditation of my heart be pleasing to you, O Lord, my rock and my redeemer."

Chapter 5

What a Crock!

My son Zach had two friends who were going to be coming over to do homework one day after school. I thought, because we were having company, it might be a good day to make a big crockpot of cheesy potato soup. I took great care to make sure I had sufficient milk, shredded cheese, and, of course, I just had to put in a bar of cream cheese. I spent time cutting up carrots to give it some color, adding onions to give it an extra zing, and using the right number of potatoes to give it substance.

I was finally ready, after all of the prep, to start cooking it in the crockpot and have it ready by 1:30 p.m., when the kids would be home from school. With all of the ingredients and the combination of the milk and water, I had all of the five-quart pot full. I was quite honestly proud of myself, knowing this meal would be covered, and we would have leftovers for another meal or two.

At around 11:00 a.m., I was about ready to do the dishes and thought I might check to see how the potatoes were softening in the crock. I was disappointed to feel they were still quite hard. I was now worried they wouldn't be soft enough in the soup by the time we needed to eat at 1:30 p.m. I decided to heat things up a bit, and that I did. I thought to myself, *If the crockpot sits in heat all day long and if I put it on the gas stove for just a little while to get it boiling, then it will advance the potatoes a bit further, and I can then put the crockpot back into the heated electrical base.*

Lifting the crock out (yes, I used hot pads), I put it on high on the gas stove and turned to wash my dishes. Brian was in another part of the house doing something, so he didn't see my ingenious idea fall into play. I had my music playing and was dancing a bit as I washed the dishes. About four minutes later, I heard a strange *pwapt* noise and dried my hands to investigate. What I saw next sent me into the quick step. On the stove my big, blue, five-quart crockpot had a hole blown out of the bottom.

Tragic as it sounds—to lose my crockpot in such a manner—a worst travesty was occurring. *All* of the liquid and ingredients from the crockpot were spilling out onto the stove and beginning to seep under all of the burners. I started yelling (the neighbors probably thought I was being killed or something), but as I yelled, I grabbed another pan to try to save what I could. As I grabbed the crockpot (yes, I used hot pads) to dump it into the bigger saucepan, the bottom of it fell out even more, spilling the rest of the five quarts over the stove and underneath. I could save none of it. Melted yellow cheese, un-melted chunks of cream cheese, and five large, cubed potatoes were now a part of the nether regions of my stove.

Leaving the dirty dishes in the sink, I now had a bigger priority. I had to figure out how to clean my stove. It was covered with what would turn into something with a sickly, sour smell if I didn't get it all taken care of. All *five* quarts had to somehow be taken care of, might I remind you.

With music still playing, I gathered the necessary equipment to start scooping out my treasured soup from the stove top and then raising the lid of the stove, like I would the hood of a car for the more daunting task of recovering it all from underneath. The song by V*Enna, *Where I Wanna Be,* was playing loudly through the speakers hooked into my iPod. With clenched teeth, I was singing loudly with the music as I scooped and cleaned. Little did I know, throughout the whole song and my interpretation of it, my husband, Brian, was standing behind me, trying to understand what in the world had just happened. I turned around and, with a startled face, just gave him a look of defeat. He asked me, "So is this really where you want to be right now?" (because of the song title).

I said to him, "No, this is *not* where I want to be right now! I ruined the soup, and now I have nothing to feed the children for our meal."

He said, "Do you need a hug?"

"Yes, please," I replied as I wrapped my arms around him and laid my head on his chest, asking, "Why do things like this always happen to me?"

"What actually *did* happen to you?" he asked.

I proceeded to tell him the whole saga, and he just stood and looked at me dumbfounded. "What would *ever* possess you to do that?"

Seriously? You're looking at my mess and dare ask me that question right now? I thought. So I told him, "A crockpot gets hot on an electric base; a crockpot gets hot on a gas stove, so it's a hot crockpot either way. Duh, that's what possessed me to do it."

He proceeded to tell me that, had I read the crockpot cooking directions (like, who actually really does that but him?), I would know the crock is made out of material that is meant to be slow-cooking, with the heat evenly dispersed. It was *not* to be put on the stove for one spot to get excessively hot and eventually crack. So, great, now I had gotten a summary of the crockpot cooking directions, my crockpot was broken, and I still had all of the soup contents seeping down through my stove.

My husband was sweet because he said so seriously, "I'm sorry that I wasn't in here to stop you. I always want to keep you from hurting yourself or doing something that will make more work for you, but I just can't be in here all of the time."

For the next hour, I used a little spoon to get to the hard-to-reach spots. I scooped little bits of liquid and chunks to be deposited into a big spoon I had right there to eventually be transferred to a big pot I placed next to the stove. Slide, scoop, deposit to big spoon; slide, scoop, deposit to big spoon, etc. When that was full, I'd dump it into the pot. I couldn't dump it into the crockpot, of course, because that was still hot, with a hole blown through the bottom of it in my sink on top of a dirty glass, which ended up breaking because of the weight of the pot. It had been my favorite glass.

The whole time, I kept thinking of all of the money I had just literally thrown away, with all of the wasted ingredients clinging to my stove. And now, one less glass. By then it was noon, and I had kids coming to my house to eat in one hour. I hadn't showered, I was sweaty and grumpy, and my house smelled like a big, yummy bowl of cheesy potato soup, which we would *not* be eating for lunch. What was I going to serve those teenagers?

I suppose when meals don't always turn out the way you want or expect them to, a good standby is always hamburgers. Hamburgers are easy to make, and, at least here in Mexico, kids love them. So, hamburgers it was. When the kids got home from school, I was showered, had gone and gotten hamburger buns and chips, and there wasn't a sign of the mishaps I'd had an hour before.

I have to admit that my grumpiness lasted the whole day. I still had to prepare for the Bible study I'd be leading the next day on words of affirmation. I decided to put that preparation off till the next morning, as I wasn't up to saying nice things to people, let alone trying to build them up. I wanted to wallow in my grumpiness. That night, as I was relaxing after my soup saga sadness, I was working on the computer when I heard, "Awe, nasty. What is all over this bottle? It's all over the bottom of the cupboard; it's sticky and gross."

Well, we don't have an oven, so under our stove is a cupboard where we store some water bottles, Brian's popcorn maker, and our cereal. I had failed to check the cupboard underneath the stove when I was cleaning my mess because why or how would any of my soup seep that low and that far down? Well, it had, and it had gotten all over everything. I couldn't wait until morning to clean it, because it would have gotten smelly.

I started to dig things out of the cupboard as they dripped liquid onto the floor. The bottoms of the cereal boxes were wet and soggy. One box of cereal only had a little bit in it, so I decided I would put it in one of my plastic containers—easy, huh? I filled the container to the top, and as I went to put the lid on, the container slipped out from under me and all of the cereal went flying all over the floor. Okay, this was the last straw. I had *had it!* I was done. I almost just left it there all over the floor and went to bed, but grumbling the whole way, I grabbed the broom and dust pan as my family watched in amazement how my day had progressed to this.

I cleaned it up in record time and, gritting my teeth, said to my family. "I've had a really hard day, and I am feeling very grumpy and mean. I am going to go to bed now so that I don't say mean or nasty things to you all. Goodnight."

So, at 8:45 p.m., I went to bed and closed myself off from the world and anyone in it. I needed an attitude adjustment, so I put myself in time out. My friend, Carol, wrote an email to me that night (knowing the struggles of my day) and said, "I'm so glad that God's mercies are new every morning, aren't you?"

And honestly, I knew the next day would be different and new and that God would have something great in store for me. Oh, by the way, the following day Brian made lunch.

The Importance of Reading the Manual

Crockpot. The Original Slow Cooker Manual.
Classic for use with the four-to-seven-quart manual slow cookers.

From page three under *Important Safeguards*:
#1 Read all instructions before using.
#9 Do not place on or near hot gas or electric burner or in a heated oven.[1]

Digging Deeper

1. It's pretty evident that reading the manual is important. The Bible is the manual to having a relationship with Christ. Read Psalm 119:105 (KJV). What does this verse tell us about reading the Bible? "Thy word is a lamp unto my feet, and a light unto my path."

2. How would your life be different if you committed to reading God's Word daily?

3. Like me not reading the crockpot instructions because I thought I knew all there was to know, what happens when we choose not to know what's in God's Word?

4. How do you respond when the bottom blows out? Have you read God's Word enough to know that He will carry you and walk beside you? Or do you feel like all is lost?

5. Make a commitment today to do what Psalm 119:11 (NIV) says. "I have hidden your word in my heart that I might not sin against you."

Chapter 6

Mexican Police, Radar Guns, and School Zones

It's never a good sign to look next to you when you are driving and see a policeman with a radar gun in his hand, motioning for you to stop. After a wonderful Bible study with my pastor's wife, I was just happily driving along. Here in Mexico, when the police stop you, you never know what may happen. As the officer came up to my car, I opened the window and said (as American as I could), "Hi." He showed me the numbers on the radar gun (which really meant nothing to me because they were in kilometers). I did, however, realize the number was much higher than what I should have been going.

He proceeded to tell me the speed limit was forty kph and that I was going sixty-nine. Oops! That's a big difference. I asked him why the speed limit was so low, and he said I was in a school zone. Oops again—didn't know there was a school nearby. I knew that my good day was now not turning out so well.

He asked if I spoke a little Spanish, and I said I did. I was proud of myself when I could communicate to him that this may be a school zone, but there was nothing marked saying so. He then pointed at four signs which should have alerted me. Well, clearly, they weren't big enough because here I sat, talking to him.

The real zinger for me was when he asked me my occupation. Ouch! I answered very honestly, "Missionary— and a very embarrassed one."

He kind of smiled. I told him I worked in a neighborhood nearby and had never known a school existed in the area. I always wondered why those little slow-down reflectors were on the road just in that area. Now I knew! He chitchatted with me for a moment. I told him I never would want to put a little school child in danger. He then said he could talk to his boss about getting me out of the ticket (of course, that's not why I made the previous comment, but it must have tugged on his heart strings). My very humble response was, "Whatever you decide will be best." I knew I was in the wrong—the numbers showed it. So I waited and waited.

In the meantime, the officer's friend, (officer number two) who had been attending another car, came up to my window and asked for my license. I showed it to him, and he started to write me a ticket. I told him that officer number one was lovingly helping me already and that I was waiting for him. "So please officer number two could you just back off?" (I didn't really say that last part.) He looked at my license and started to explain that *when* I get my ticket, they will take away my license until I pay a fine.

By then, officer number one had returned and was telling me how much tickets cost and opened the book, as if *he* were going to write me a ticket. So much for talking to his boss about forgoing giving me one. At that moment, he asked how much money I had with me. Fortunately, I had nothing. I was able to show him my empty wallet. I think they both wanted me to pay them something right there. Were these the bribes I had heard so much about? No way was I going to do that, but I wanted my license back.

My next option was to go to a police station to pay the speeding ticket fine. So there I sat, on a main street in my city, officer number two still holding my license, not even knowing there was a school nearby or what the speed limit really was, and he expected me to find a police station? I told them both I had no idea where there was a police station. I really think they didn't know what to do with me, so he handed me back my license. Police officer number one said I had better slow it down, now that I knew where the school was in this neighborhood.

I gave the officers my thanks for truly granting me mercy this day. And they had. I was guilty, and only mercy could have saved me from a ticket.

Digging Deeper

1. Are you truly aware of the things are around you? Stop for a moment and really take it all in. Do you notice the birds chirping in the trees or your kids wanting you to play with them or the struggles of people in your city or the older person who walks by your house daily to whom you could speak?

2. Nehemiah 1: 2–4 (NIV) says, "Hanani, one of my brothers, came from Judah with some other men, and I questioned them about the Jewish remnant that had survived the exile, and also about Jerusalem. They said to me, 'Those who survived the exile and are back in the province are in great trouble and disgrace. The wall of Jerusalem is broken down, and its gates have been burned with fire.' When I heard these things, I sat down and wept. For some days I mourned and fasted and prayed before the God of heaven."

3. Nehemiah clearly was aware of the trouble in the "land in which his ancestors were buried," and he wanted to help be part of the solution. If you read the entire book of Nehemiah, you will see that he became part of the solution and headed up the rebuilding of the wall around Jerusalem.

4. This next week, let me challenge you to not just "drive along happily," like I did in the story above, but to really see what is around you and determine if you need to be part of the solution. Once you see a need you can help fill, list it below.

a.

b.

c.

d.

Chapter 7

Tarantulas in the Toilet

Since living in Mexico, I have had to learn to adjust to the differences in climate, foliage, bugs, etc. Having lived in Michigan for a long while, I had gotten used to the wet, humid, cloudy, rainy, snowy part of life. I just knew, in Michigan in the summertime, there would be a lot of mosquitoes. I knew I would see daddy longlegs spiders, and I knew that, occasionally, I would see a garter snake. As a teenager, I stepped on one with my bare feet. Kind of slithery but it couldn't harm me. But in Mexico, there are cockroaches and poisonous spiders; there are coyotes in the desert, jackrabbits with big, giant ears, and several types of poisonous snakes. I'm really not partial to any of these, with the exception of the cute rabbits with their funny ears.

One evening, I came face to face (or should I say, butt to face) with one of these creatures I don't care for. My heart almost stopped, and even my scream stuck in my throat. It was the annual ladies' retreat at the church conference ranch. I am very familiar with this ranch because I went down over twenty years ago—early in its formation—with a mission team to help with its construction.

The ranch is a beautiful place for retreat, and to me, it's like a mini-resort in the midst of seven hundred acres of desert. People have worked hard to make paths lined by stones and areas clear of jumping cactuses so that every step you take isn't so painful. (Of course, it should be no big surprise that these jumping cactuses still fly across the path when they see my leg or my foot.) There is a very large area designed as a walking path that winds through the desert. It allows visitors to see the different trees and the Saguaro cactuses (the ones with arms that only live in the Sonoran desert), birds, an occasional big-eared bunny, and possibly even a traversing hairy tarantula. It's actually a delightful area and full of God's majesty, extending too the chain of beautiful mountains in the distance.

When I am at the ladies' retreat, I choose to stay in the missionary trailer, which is a ways out from the main hub of things. I do this because I am really grumpy if I don't get my sleep. I found out, after staying with the ladies the first year I went, many of them just don't sleep. They talk and laugh until two or three o'clock in the morning. Once they are asleep, the next set of women are up at 5:00 a.m., sitting outside of my door, telling stories and laughing like it's the middle of the day. Now I'm all for talking and laughing and spending time together, but when I'm ready for bed I want it quiet. So I figured, for everyone involved, I would put my all into the women during the day and go to my 1970s aluminum-sided fortress at night. Of course, by the time all of the activities of the day are done it is well past 10:00 p.m., and I am ready for bed.

This particular evening, I headed back to the trailer, grabbed my flashlight, and walked to the building a few yards away to brush my teeth and use the bathroom one last time for the night. As I walked into the room that had a sink and two bathroom stalls I turned on the light, and the bulb blew out. I was very glad I had brought my flashlight. I brushed my teeth and then gently laid my flashlight on the counter to shine some light into the stall while I used the facilities. I wanted to be able to see where the actual toilet was, without having to feel around for it. So I left the stall door open and proceeded to sit down to, well, do what you do when you're sitting in the bathroom.

When I stood up, I turned around to flush, and the light hit the inside of the bowl just so. That's when I saw it. A big, giant, hairy, size-of-a-car tarantula was sitting inside the toilet bowl. It was alive. I screamed in my mind, but nothing, I mean, no sound was going to squeak out of this freaked-out lady. It just couldn't make its way out. I stopped, stunned, and looked at it. It looked at me, and then I did what any freaked-out lady who'd seen a tarantula in a dark toilet would do. I reached down and flushed that baby. And I flushed it good. I hoped it flushed all the way to Arizona because I wanted it gone and away from me. When I left the stall to wash my hands and was finally able to speak out loud, I said, "Thank You, Lord, that it didn't bite me in the butt."

You see, I was the only one out that way by the trailers at that moment, and I would have had to go back up to the main area, find someone, and try to explain in my imperfect Spanish that I had been bitten by a tarantula ... in the butt. Because tarantulas are poisonous, the ladies would have had to take me to the town hospital. And here, my mind starts to be thankful over and over again because I am picturing the college intern who has to work the night shift (thinking, *surely no one will be coming in with anything serious*) having to ask me to pull down my pants and look at my backside. I was just imagining the sheer awkwardness and embarrassment! Oh, the joy that Mr. T had been flushed before he could take a chunk out of the large, pale thing that hung just inches from him.

As I walked back to my trailer, I kept thanking God for His kindness and mercy to me that night. I slept well, though still a little squeamish over what I had experienced. That just doesn't go quickly out of one's mind.

The following morning, I was having breakfast with my Mexican friends. I relayed the story to them and thought for sure they would have the utmost concern for what could have happened to their precious missionary friend. Instead, one gal said to me, "But Laura, think of it from the tarantula's perspective."

She then proceeded to put her hands up, as if to stop gallons of water that might fall on her. The other women at the table began to laugh so hard they couldn't even eat.

Before we came to Mexico to live, someone told us that Mexicans are very serious and don't really have a sense of humor. After all the time spent here with my dear friends, I would have to say that statement is an untrue one. Oh, yes, my Mexican friends can be very serious, but when they get to laughing and joking, there is no stopping them. Only they would be thinking of the tarantula's perspective. That was the last thing from my mind. I was happy to give my friends something to laugh about that morning and sure was thankful the tarantula was perhaps blinded for a slight moment after being *hit*, so he couldn't bite me.

Digging Deeper

1. Name a time when something happened that paralyzed you with fear.

2. Sometimes fear doesn't necessarily paralyze us, but we always have this underlying feeling of concern about it. Maybe it's fear of heights, fear of closed-in places, fear of snakes or spiders, fear of not being safe in our homes. So how do you deal with such fears on a day to day basis?

3. I love what Deuteronomy 31:6 (NIV) says. "Be strong and courageous. Do not be afraid or terrified because of them, for the LORD your God goes with you; he will never leave you nor forsake you."

4. At the time this verse was written, the Israelites were going to a new land, nervous because they heard there were giants there; they had honest fear of the unknown. Write down a time when you had fear of the unknown.

5. No matter what fear comes our way, we know that God goes with us. I was pretty fearful of what could have happened with the tarantula at the conference ranch. Thankfully, nothing did happen. But I am confident that, had my little friend taken a small bite (though I'd have been embarrassed) God would have been with me every step of the way. Why? Because He promised! Can you trust Him to take away your fears?

Chapter 8

One Season Following Another

I recall clearly one day, after about three years of marriage, when my husband, Brian, sat me down and said he was ready to have children. I tried to contain myself, but I was seriously freaking out inside. My lands! *I* was a child; how could I have children? I was just shy of twenty-six—that's way too young to be a mother. What if they throw up? Gross! How would I ever manage it? That throw-up business made me *not* want children.

Many other questions began to flood my mind. How do you bathe such a little thing? I didn't know. How do you change a diaper? I didn't know. I hadn't been around babies or little children much, so the thought of being responsible for one almost gave me a heart attack. I did want children, and I knew it was time. I figured that God had helped me through the other things of life enough to trust Him to help me through vomit, nights with no sleep, and putting diapers on a squirming child.

I never ever imagined the joy a child could bring. Don't get me wrong; when they say new mothers quickly forget the pain of childbirth, I think the *theys* are lying because I surely remember. Oh, yes, I remember. However, the pure joy of seeing your child for the first time is something I was not expecting. How I fell in love in an instant is a miracle beyond belief. At that point, you don't care if they throw up on you; you'll clean it with joy because of that love. If they poop all over their newborn outfits, it's okay because that love will make you change them into a new outfit just given to you at your baby shower. Joy—unending joy.

In an instant, it was eighteen years later, and I recall the days I sent my two sons off to their new lives. It happened two years apart (thankfully, so I could have a break from the crying). With our first, Brian and I stood on our porch in Michigan, where we were living for a year during home assignment from the mission field. We stood there in silence as we watched our oldest son, Mitchell, drive away in the little black Stratus. Before he left for his freshman year of college, he'd been living and working an hour away from us at a Christian summer camp. We knew, at that moment, life would change—things would be different. When he came home, it would be to visit and do laundry. He wouldn't be living with us day to day.

I began to cry as I watched the tail lights round the corner. I was devastated. My mother's heart went into mourning, and we had to find out what life would be with one less child in the house. Two years later, I stood in an airport, hugging my second son, Zachary, goodbye, watching him go through the security. I didn't leave until I could see him no longer. Tears rolled down my face as I slowly waved farewell, and he faded into (what seemed to be) nothingness. My heart broke once again. I made it to the airport bathroom just in time to close the stall door and bawl my eyes out.

When we were leaving the airport, we heard voices yell, "Brian, Laurie!" and it was David and Yvonne Roller. This couple had lived in the basement apartment below me in college when they were home from the mission field. They later became our bosses when we went to the mission field. They are just precious people—so pure, kind, and caring. They were heading back home after being in Mexico for meetings. Yvonne knew we were dropping Zach off to go to Michigan, and when I approached her, she just embraced me and let me cry on her shoulder. I was so touched as she cried right along with me, whispering such gentle, comforting things. I felt God had put them there at such a perfect time. (I love how God does that!)

We walked out of the sliding doors to the view of cactuses, knowing that, yet again, our lives would change and that we would have to adjust to the new normal of having only one child in the house instead of two. When we had regained composure and had gotten into the car, I turned to our daughter, Emily, and said, "I think it might be best if you stay and live with us forever."

However, we knew even that wasn't right because, in four years, we would be doing the same thing with her. We would send her off to do what God had planned for her. Though our hearts would feel like they were breaking, we would know that it would be right because she, along with the boys, loved the Lord and desired to serve Him. What parent could ask for more?

It's been just about a week since I hugged Zachary goodbye at the airport. It's fresh. I miss him already. I miss him being downstairs, watching the news or *Stargate* when I get up in the morning. I miss bringing him coffee and having him say every single time, "I didn't expect this!" I miss passing by his room and hearing the clinking of the Legos from his latest detailed creation of a three-foot long battleship he had planned out in his mind the day before and then took the time and patience to create it.

And Mitchell? It's been two years, and I still miss him. He's the one who would always come up and say, "Mom, you look like you need a hug," and then engulf me in his huge arms and squeeze me tightly. I miss his sensitivity and awareness of things most teenage boys don't have a clue about.

It does get easier because I suppose you learn to live with the changes. I never imagined when I first held those two boys in my arms how the time would fly by so quickly. I always remember older moms saying the cliché, "Love them while you can because they'll be gone before you know it." Or, when they are acting like horrible terrors and you want to pull your hair out and send them to time out for a whole day, an older mother would sweep in behind saying, "I'd give anything to have my kids at that stage again." In place of smacking her for saying that at completely the wrong time, I remember just smiling and thinking *why don't you take them for a day then?*

I've loved my children at every stage—even the teenager stage. I just didn't think it would all fly by in the blink of an eye. I have so much more to do, so many parenting skills I need to go back and correct, so many things I would do differently. But then again, don't we all? If I kept them home for the rest of their lives, they would never be able to flourish and pursue the things God has for them. What mom would truly want that? I see God using my children, and I want them to have the freedom to spread their wings and go for it. It's not easy living in another country with my boys so far away. What if they need their mommy? What if they get sick? I have to trust God that He has brought us this far and trust His promise that He loves my children more than I do.

When I was a senior in high school, I played Golde in the musical *Fiddler on the Roof.* I remember the song I had to sing called *Sunrise, Sunset.* It was about a couple looking back at their young lives—when they got married and had children—and how time went by so quickly that, before they knew it, their daughter was getting married. They realized they had gotten older but didn't remember it happening. (I feel this way often.) Last week, before dropping Zach off at the airport, the lyrics of that song I sang over thirty years ago kept going through my mind. Honestly, it had more significance in the real life of today than the play acting I did as a high school student.

Digging Deeper

1. Read Deuteronomy 11:18–19 (NIV). "Fix these words of mine in your hearts and minds; tie them as symbols on your hands and bind them on your foreheads. Teach them to your children, talking about them when you sit at home and when you walk along the road, when you lie down and when you get up."

    a. What four things are we supposed to do with the Word of the Lord?

    b. When are you supposed to teach the Word of the Lord to your children?

2. What would happen if we never let our children grow into the people God wanted them to be?

3. As mothers, we are far from perfect. What do you need to do today to make the most of the time you have with your children and to teach them the ways of the Lord? Make a list of at least five different things you can do.

Chapter 9

Lessons Learned on the Ball Field

I really enjoy sports. As a child I would go out and play football with the boys any chance I could get. They told me that I was pretty good too ... for a girl. I remember twenty-minute recesses in fifth grade, catching football passes that no other girl could catch and feeling pretty good that I could keep up with the boys.

As I grew older, I spent most of my summers at the tennis courts, hitting the ball back and forth, back and forth against a wood backboard. I also spent a lot of time playing softball, which I loved. Every summer, I was on one of the rec teams of the city, and with my strong throwing arm, I enjoyed some success. As I went through high school, I had to make a decision to play softball on the school team or to be in the school musicals. Because I also loved to sing, I opted for the musicals because I knew that I could play ball in the summer.

When I went to Spring Arbor College my freshman year (now Spring Arbor University), I lived on a dorm floor where many of the girls were softball players. I didn't request it; it just ended up that way. My suitemate was there on a pitching scholarship, and many others received scholarships to play. As tryouts neared, my friends told me I should just try out. "Go in as a walk-on (one not given a scholarship) because it's better to try and not make it than to not try. Plus, we could all spend more time together if you made it," they said.

I knew it was going to be a longshot but liked the idea of spending more time with my friends, and playing softball at the same time would be a huge bonus. So why not? I made the decision to try out. If anything, practicing with the team would get me in good shape.

We returned to college in January, after Christmas break, for conditioning. This was what the team members did before they even picked up a softball. How hard could that be? We'd run a little, lift weights, etc. After day one, I almost died. This was not summer rec softball anymore; this was the real thing, and I had been run like a dog! The only time the gym was available was at 6:00 a.m. So every morning, my friends, Rhonda, Tonie, and Cherilyn would walk past my door at the end of the floor, tap on it, and without a word, we would all walk one flight down to where Fish and Jodi were waiting for us to continue as a group to the fieldhouse in the cold darkness.

We would start with stretches—in the attempt to wake up our bodies—and then it was like things all went in double time. We would go to the stairs (thirty-two of them, to be exact) and we would run for what seemed like forever, doing sprints up and down and up and down. We then would go to the gym and do killers—not just on the basketball court lines, but across the whole gym. We would do intervals of twenty-five-yard sprints and then other creative sprints I never knew existed.

All of this running was physical torment. Why? Because I hate to run. Oh, it's not just a dislike; it's hatred. I know I shouldn't use that word, but nothing else describes the intensity of the evil thoughts I have about running. I must have been crazy to even think of attempting this, but I did it. My body would ache, my muscles would hurt, and I would walk to class afterward looking (and feeling) like an aching, slumped-over old lady.

The reward of all of the conditioning was that we knew we would soon be picking up the balls and bats and working with them. I remember playing in the gym because it was too cold and snowy to play outside. There were the sheer joys of being able to throw that ball across the whole gym and to be able to hit that fastball coming off the batting machine. I was hooked. I loved it, and this was just the preliminaries. I hadn't even made the team yet.

Most people knew they were on the team because they weren't walk-ons; they had been asked to play on scholarship. However, my story was different, so I was on pins and needles the day we were going to be given the roster. I was so nervous. I wasn't fast, like the other girls, didn't have the ball-handling skills they had, and my batting ability left a lot to be desired. Not positive things when you want to make a college team. Coach Deb brought me into her office to tell me the news. Oh, the nerves, the anticipation—I was sick to my stomach. She said, "Congratulations, Laurie; you are now a member of the Spring Arbor College softball team."

Really? Me? She told me I had a lot of work to do, that I had a great arm, but mostly I had a really good attitude, and that's what she wanted on her team. I was stunned. I was excited. I wanted to hug her. I couldn't wait to go back and tell my friends I had made the team. What a joyous day for me.

I spent most of that season on the bench, cheering my team on, but improving in my skills and strategies of the game. The positive thing about being in the dugout is you can listen to what the coaches are strategizing about during the game and watch them work the plan to fulfill it. When I did play, I was put in right field (probably because not many balls went there). My arm was good, and I could, if needed, throw the ball to home plate to get a runner out. There was one especially memorable play for me that year in right field.

It was a cold day when I thought my fingers might freeze. There were two outs, and I was in ready position, just waiting for the ball to come my way. The sound of the bat cracking was loud, and the ball was coming right to me but was coming very shallow. I ran up, grabbed it on one hop, and with all of my might, threw it to our first baseman. Normally, when a ball gets hit to the outfield and it hops, it's a sure bet that the runner will go safely to first base. Not this time. She was out! It was an incredible play. I actually threw the ball to just the right spot for the first baseman to stretch and snatch it before the runner got to the bag. It was one of those *hip, hip, hooray* moments, where everyone is excited and celebrating, and you run into the dugout feeling on top of the world.

Here's what I found out later from my coach's best friend, who had been in the dugout with her during that play. My coach—dear, kind, Deb Varland—teared up, smiled, and said to her friend something like, "That's my girl. She did it, I knew she could. She was a walk-on this season, and she did it."

I almost think I was more excited hearing that than I was making the play. I had so much respect for my coach and for the help and encouragement she had given me that I felt like I had just been voted Most Valuable Player.

Our team went to national championships that year and placed fifth in the nation for NCAA. I would like to say I made wonderful plays in aiding the team to get to that spot, but I didn't. In fact, during the national championships I wasn't able to play because I was so sick. What I learned most that year really had less to do with softball but more to do with what it meant to be part of a team and to build a winning team with others. I learned what it meant to have a coach who believes in you, even when you don't believe in yourself. The confidence my coach had in me that year and what she taught me about relationships became a springboard for how I was to live my life.

Digging Deeper

1. Have you ever had someone in your life with great confidence in you, and you wondered what he or she saw in you that you couldn't see in yourself? Share your story below.

2. In what ways were you encouraged by this person or others to be better in your life?

3. First Thessalonians 5:11 (TLB) says, "So encourage each other and build each other up, just as you are already doing."

4. Does the above verse describe you as a person? Do you encourage others?

5. How can you make a difference in others' lives by believing in them and maybe giving them a chance they wouldn't normally have?

Chapter 10

Back-Pedaling Blues

After loving and learning how to better play the game and build deep relationships with team members in my first year of college softball, I played on the team for the remainder of the time I was in college. I was again in right field, and we were playing an away game at Oakland University. Twenty-five years later, I can still remember the stadium, the grass, the dirt, the crowd, my team, and how I felt riding the bus home after the game. The ball field was positioned in such a way that, for the spectators to see well, they were able to stand alongside the right field line. I could turn and talk to the people if I wanted to as I was standing out there. I was all decked-out with my ball hat and sunglasses, ready for anything to come at me.

Now, a common teaching technique for outfielders is to know when a ball is coming toward you, you turn and run, always keeping your eyes on the ball, but you *never* backpedal. Backpedaling will get you in trouble, as I soon was going to find out. The crack of the bat, a high pop fly coming straight at me, the crowd lined along the fence, and three runners on base. Yes, bases were loaded!

Feeling nervous with anticipation of getting that ball in my glove, I began to backpedal (are you seeing where this is going?). Suddenly, my cleats got all tangled up and I fell, running backward. As I hit the ground, I watched the ball fly straight over my head. There was a moment when everything turned into slow motion. I heard the crowd slowing laughing; I heard my teammates yelling, "Geeeettttt uuuuupppp, Laaaaauuuurriiieee!"

Then it all came back quickly, in a whirlwind of laughter. The yelling, the screaming, and me getting up and running to the fence for the ball—the ball just sitting there, waiting for me to get it. Even when I got to the ball, I fumbled it because I was so embarrassed at what had just occurred. In the meantime, one run passed home plate, two runs passed home plate, three runs passed home plate, and I finally threw the ball to the infield to hold the hitter at third base. We finally got out of the inning, with no help from me, I might add.

Walking to the dugout was like the walk down the long corridor to the principal's office (yes, I've done that too, on occasion). It was lonely and quiet. When I got into the dugout, my team members didn't say a word; they just looked at me, trying not to smile. Finally, because I knew it was killing them not to, I told them they could laugh. The whole dugout was in an uproar with laughter and smiles, jabbing at me for my little *accident* out in right field.

My coach? Not so much. As I recall, I had a replacement for the next inning, and we never did recover from that play. We lost the game. The bus ride home was long, and I was filled with a real lack of self-esteem. I asked myself *Why would I ever try out for a team that I had no business being on? Why did my friends laugh at me when I had tried so hard?* I was feeling very sorry for myself, not to mention seeing the slow motion laughter of the spectators in my mind.

It wasn't long until my teammates came around me, one by one, and encouraged me to keep trying and not to give up. This was the kind of team of which I was a part. I may not have been the pitcher that struck out many batters or the hitter that slammed the ball over the fence, but I was the girl with the good arm who could cheer my team on with the best of them. My role was a different one. I was an outfielder that caught fly balls and, on more than one occasion, blew it in a big way. But I was part of a team. We each had our own jobs to do. Just like in the body of Christ, we don't all have gifts in the same areas. We use our gifts, others' use their gifts, and we make up a whole team to work together.

Just imagine if I hadn't been in right field that day. Sure, I had my backpedal blunder, but if it had just been an empty spot out there, someone else would have had to scramble to get that ball. Maybe her arm wouldn't have had the power to throw a ball to third base, and yet another run would have been scored.

You see, friend, you are gifted. Will you step out and use it or will you, if you backpedal and fall once, leave an empty hole where your gift is needed? You are an important part of the body of Christ. Stay in the game!

Digging Deeper

1. Ephesians 4:16 (NIV) says, "From him the whole body, joined and held together by every supporting ligament, grows and builds itself up in love, as each part does its work."

2. What is the gift(s) God has given you to use in the body of Christ?

3. What happens if, on Christ's team, we give up and don't do our parts by using our gifts?

4. Do you know someone on your *team* who is struggling to continue using his or her gifts? How can you be a supporting ligament to that person?

Chapter 11

Hubcaps in the Desert ... Seriously?

Those who have been on a short-term mission trip will understand well the impact it has on a person. There is no way to remain the same person after experiencing this type of ministry. In 1992, I had the opportunity to take my first short-term mission trip. My husband, Brian, and I led a group of teens from our church conference in Michigan to the newly-purchased camp of the Free Methodist Church in Sonora, Mexico called *Rancho Betania*.

There we were, put in the middle of the desert on 700 acres of nothing but brush, shrub, cactus, snakes, and long-eared jackrabbits. I was in awe of God's creation—the mountains, the desert. Everything was amazing for me to see for the first time. It was so pure, so untainted. I was taking it all in every minute and loving it. I couldn't believe the night sky and how crystal clear it was. You could see a vast number of stars in any direction. Morning would come quickly, and I was soon to be impressed by the heat of the sun. By 6:00 a.m., we had to be out of our tent because the heat was so intense it literally melted the gel deodorant I had in my bag and would have probably melted us too if we had stayed inside. It surely was a trip to see and experience new, beautiful, and wondrous things.

I never could have imagined myself working so hard in that 110-degree heat every day. It was a joy to see the team working together, building, pouring cement, shoveling dirt, building forms, etc. And I never could have imagined in all my life having to drink so much water. There were bumps and bruises along the way, but the thrill of the work and serving others overshadowed those little hurts and motivated me to continue on.

One day on our lunch break, I was somehow at the very back of the line. (That, in and of itself, seems odd, as eating is my hobby.) I must have been trying to communicate in Spanish with one of the Mexicans, and that endeavor held me back from the group. All of the teens and Brian had already gotten their meals and had been seated underneath the canopy provided to shield us from the scalding sun. As I was still going through the line getting my food, one of the teens turned to Brian and said, "Now I don't want this to sound bad, but does Laurie hurt herself … a lot?"

As Brian started to answer, he looked up to see me walk from the food line to the canopy. With my tray in hand and a smile on my face as I walked, my foot landed right inside a hubcap. The hubcap flipped up and hit me so hard on the shin that I began jumping around, hootin' and hollerin'(never spilling anything from my tray, I'd like to add). At that point, everyone at the table who had just heard the young man's question to Brian started laughing. Here I was, hobbling in pain, and they were laughing. I couldn't believe it. To this day, I'm still shocked that there was a hubcap in the middle of the Sonoran desert. Why in the world was it there? I never did find out.

I proceeded to limp my way to the other end of the canopy to find my seat so I could eat my lunch. I was still put out that everyone was laughing. As I rounded the corner to take my seat, I tripped over the stake holding up the canopy. The sound of laughter at that point was at a high decibel. I was starting to get a little frustrated (no, actually mad) that they all could be so heartless—and my husband too.

As they finally quieted down, Brian answered the young man with, "I believe you have your answer." He then proceeded to tell me how I had literally walked (rather tripped) into giving a very real answer to a very serious question.

I haven't seen a hubcap in the middle of the desert since, and my shins hope to never see one lying on the ground anywhere again. I wasn't expecting to have to look down and to beware of hubcaps sticking out of the ground. Normally in the desert you just find cactuses, trees, and lots of dirt. If I'd have known it back then, I would have grabbed that authentic Mexican hubcap, brought it home, and sold it on Craigslist!

Digging Deeper

1. How do you respond when something happens unexpectedly?

2. Acts 20:9 (TLB) says, "As Paul spoke on and on, a young man named Eutychus, sitting on the windowsill, became very drowsy. Finally, he fell sound asleep and dropped three stories to his death below."

3. Imagine you are there, intently listening to Jesus. What was the unexpected event that happened?

4. I love the wording in The Living Bible because it says that Paul spoke "on and on." It's a huge indication to me that this teenager had no idea Paul was going to speak *that* long, and he unexpectedly fell asleep. Sadly, the consequences of falling asleep were much more than the whiplash we might experience by falling asleep during a sermon in our church. Check out what happens next as you read Acts 20:10–11 (TLB). "Paul went down, bent over him, and took him into his arms. 'Don't worry,' he said, 'he's alive!' Then they all went back upstairs, shared in the Lord's Supper, and ate together. Paul continued talking to them until dawn, and then he left."

5. As if falling out a window wasn't unexpected enough, what does Paul do?

6. Some unexpected things that happen in our lives may seem like the end of the road. (It certainly had looked like it for Eutychus.) Just remember, in our unexpected circumstances we have a God who can do things that to us seem to be impossible and unexpected.

Chapter 12

Weren't You Ever Taught as a Child *Not* to Go with Strangers?

Driving—I don't particularly like to do it, but I need to do it. My driving now consists mostly of city driving to get groceries, take the kids to and from school, and participate in ministry activities. When we lived in small-town America, I could drive on country roads and just enjoy the ride. I never really paid much attention to the speedometer because I just drove.

Here in the city, I also just drive. I suppose my method isn't a very good one because I've had family and friends describe my driving as scary, crazy, distracted, and nerve-wracking. Living in a large Mexican city, if you want to get to where you want to go, sometimes you have to be a little more aggressive than you would on a road surrounded by cornfields. With my personality as a competitor and a go-getter, I caught on quickly how to do it. So where some women are afraid to drive in the city, my motto is "Bring it on!" (even though I truly do despise it). It's a means to an end.

Some driving days are better than others. You kind of sense you are either in a groove or just stuck behind a brick truck or an old, beat-up car, spitting smoke in your face. There was one sunny fall morning on which I had to run some errands before I was to go and speak to a group of women in the afternoon. Things were going my way. I was getting green lights and didn't have abnormally slow people in front of me. I was just "getting 'er done." I had been in one store, asking about some information on ordering T-shirts for the church. People were standing around talking, and one of them was a police officer. He was chit-chatting with one of the workers. I got what I needed and left.

I pulled out and drove along in the four-lane traffic at the speed all of the other cars were going. In my mirror I saw a police motorcycle with his lights on. This wasn't a really big deal to me, as the police here in the city always drive with their lights on. I've yet to figure out why. He pulled up beside me and motioned me over. *Are you kidding me? I'm getting pulled over? For what?* were the thoughts running through my mind.

He came up to my window and told me he pulled me over because I was going too fast. (Remember, I said before that I just drive, and since I was driving with traffic, I figured that I was fine.) Apparently, my explanation of going with the speed of traffic didn't fly because he proceeded to explain to me that in Mexico, they don't use that law. Great! Here comes a ticket.

Then he asked me an odd question. "So you are pricing T-shirts, huh? I was back at the store with you when you were asking prices."

I replied with a little confusion, "Um, yes, I'm looking for shirts."

He said, "My cousin owns this place that prints shirts, and he can give you a much better deal than that guy back there. If you want, I can take you there."

Well, always looking for a good deal, I said, "Great, let's go!"

He wasn't interested in giving me a ticket; he was interested in stopping me so he could take me to his cousin.

So off we drove, with me being escorted by the police. I felt like I was something special. We started driving into neighborhoods away from where the stores are located, weaving in and out of little roads. Then the thought hit me. *Oh, my lands! He is going to take me somewhere and kill me!* Now what was I going to do? They say there are many corrupt police working alongside the drug cartel, and I suddenly had horrible things running through my mind. I didn't know exactly where I was, so speeding away from him was not going to work.

As I drove, I grabbed my purse and emptied out my money, my credit cards, my driver's license—everything I could think of they might steal. I stuck these items deep into the consol of the van, and when we stopped at a stop sign, I quickly turned the car off, grabbed the keys, and locked the consol. Now my purse was empty of the important things, so if they were going to kill me they wouldn't be able to use my credit cards. (Of course, I thought later how dumb that was because they'd never be able to identify my body either. But you don't think of those things in the heat of the moment.)

We finally pulled down a dirt road and up to a warehouse that was not really near any houses. Did I say a warehouse? It was like a bad movie. The police officer stopped his bike, with a smile on his face, and motioned for me to come with him. "Dear Jesus, I don't know why I do the things I do or fall into the situations I fall into, but please help my family to at least be able to identify my body and give me a proper burial after these people in the warehouse torture and kill me." I quietly said under my breath.

We walked slowly into the warehouse, and the police officer greeted everyone with a smile and then took me to a little office. *That's where it would happen*, I thought. *That's where I would die. O Lord, what about my family? What about the T-shirts I promised to order for the church? What about ...*

"So my cousin tells me you are looking to order some shirts. Well, he brought you to the right place. We do printing for all of the major companies here in the city, like Ford Motor Company, University of Sonora, etc."

Really? I thought. *This was a legit business? I wasn't going to die? Yippee!*

I started to relax and, amidst my shaking, tried to be professional. I shared with the guys what I was looking for, and they gave me a really great deal. The police officer was right when he stopped me. His cousin really could do better than the other guy! Not only did he give me a good deal, but because we were talking about the hats they printed for the professional baseball team here in the city, he gave me a hat. Not only did I not die, but I got a good deal on shirts and a free, awesome *Naranjeros* hat.

As I returned to my car, I realized there are kind people in this world. I'm not saying that you should follow a stranger down strange roads to a big warehouse, but sometimes we need to give people the benefit of the doubt. I drove away, thankful for my *police altercation* and, of course, my free hat.

Digging Deeper

1. Have you ever trusted someone too quickly and then realized you had made the wrong choice? How did that work out for you? Did it end up getting you in trouble, or did things work out for you like they did in my story above?

2. Many know the Bible story of Samson and Delilah. He has this great strength that no one knows how to stop and she keeps trying to get him to tell her the secret. The problem is she can't be trusted. Over and over in Judges 16 she tries to trick him. In Judges 16:15–17 (NIV), she again manipulates him into trusting her by saying,

   > "How can you say, 'I love you,' when you won't confide in me? This is the third time you have made a fool of me and haven't told me the secret of your great strength." With such nagging she prodded him day after day until he was sick to death of it. So he told her everything. "No razor has ever been used on my head," he said, "because I have been a Nazirite dedicated to God from my mother's womb. If my

head were shaved, my strength would leave me, and I would become as weak as any other man."

3. If you don't know the story, then you can probably guess what happened from there. She lied to him (big surprise), shaved his head, and handed him over.

   a. Then verse 21 says, "The Philistines seized him, gouged out his eyes and took him down to Gaza. Binding him with bronze shackles, they set him to grinding grain in the prison."

   b. Samson made a poor choice; he had trusted someone who was untrustworthy. What would make him do this over and over again?

4. God puts people along our path every day. Are we careful to think through whom we will or will not trust with the important things of our lives? William Shakespeare said it well in *All's Well that Ends Well*: "Love all, trust a few, do wrong to none." [2]

Chapter 13

Making Friends with the Police Twice in One Day

I suppose you would say that I have a need for speed. I am not a very patient person and like to quickly get to where I am going. I don't like to putz around and do the Sunday drive thing. Just get me there. After my morning spent following a strange policeman to a warehouse, I had to go home and get ready to speak at a gathering of the ladies from our eight Free Methodist churches here in Hermosillo. I was thrilled to have been asked and was excited to be able to share what God had put on my heart.

I grabbed my Bible, coffee, purse, and the bag of chips I was asked to bring and walked out the door. I had just enough time to get across town and pick up my friend before we headed to the church. I decided to drive down one of the less-traveled roads that cut across town because I figured it would be quicker. There were no cars around me, and I was enjoying my music, my coffee, and the beautiful day. And that's when it happened. I rounded a corner and señor motorcycle policeman had radar pointed right at me. Of course, I looked down at my speedometer and, yep, I was going too fast. He directed me to pull into this little area where, apparently, they always like to stop cars. I can't recall if I started praying, crying, or what; I just knew I had been going too fast, and I was going to be late if I didn't get going soon.

The officer came up to my window and asked if I knew how fast I was going. I said I was going about forty, and he said, "No, you were actually going 103."

So the speed limit was forty kilometers, which is like twenty-five miles per hour. *Does anyone really go that slowly through there?* I thought to myself but didn't dare say to him. I told him, in actuality, I *was* going forty. He smiled and said, "Mam, forty miles per hour is *not* the same as forty kilometers."

Okay, so that didn't work. He asked for my license and registration, and I gave it to him. He told me very clearly that he would be writing me a ticket. Here is where I started to scramble—I was going to try anything ... well, except lying and crying. I can't cry at will. All I could think of was getting out of this ticket.

I tried to stall him and talk about why he shouldn't give me a ticket. He just wasn't buying it. (I really didn't expect he would.) Then I saw them—the potato chips on the passenger seat. I knew I had one last chance. I'd heard that the Mexican police take bribes, so I was going to try one. I was seriously going to offer the officer a bribe. I had no money, but everybody likes a good potato chip, right? So I picked up the chips, smiled, and asked, "How about if you don't give me a ticket, and I will give you this bag of chips?"

I realized that it was not the thing to do. Oops! He, with a smile on his face, told me how, if I had a credit card I could pay right then and there by using his little credit card scanning machine. Wow, it was my lucky day! He started to walk over to get the machine, and I said, "Wait, please. If you give me a ticket, then I will have to tell my husband, and then he will ask why I was going so fast and ... and ..."

We were now fifteen minutes into me unsuccessfully trying to get out of this ticket. The husband card didn't work either. Boy was I in trouble. He proceeded to start writing the ticket.

I knew I had one last card to play. It wasn't a pretty card, and I was not proud of myself for having to use it, but I did because I desperately didn't want this ticket. The brother of my very close friend here in Mexico is a motorcycle cop in this city. I was about to be a name-dropper for the second time in one day. As the officer was starting to write, I casually said, "Oh, I have a friend who is a motorcycle cop here in Hermosillo; you may know him. His name is ..."

Suddenly, he stopped writing, and with a smile, yelled over to his buddy, "Hey, this lady knows 'Thumper,' which, I suppose, was my friend's nickname (to protect his anonymity, it is not his real nickname).

They both started laughing and were telling me yes, they knew him and asked how I knew him. I proudly told them my close connection to him. How awesome was that? At this point, I knew I had hit the nail on the head and was thinking it was pretty *awesome*. He put his clipboard away, stuck his pen in his pocket, smiled, and said to me, "Slow down, and have a nice day."

Incredible. Just by saying this person's name I had gotten out of the ticket. I wanted to get out and do a happy dance but thought it might be a little too celebratory. So what I did next surprised even me. I reached over and grabbed the bag of chips I had offered before and said, "You guys still want a bag of chips?" They looked at each other, smiled, and said, "Yeah, sure."

Glowing in my *win*, I pulled away from them and realized I was fifteen minutes late in picking up my friend. I had farther to drive, and as I got to thinking about the situation I had just been faced with, I started to feel guilty and disappointed in myself; I had been conniving ... horrible. I called my close friend, who was teaching a class at the time, and told her how terrible I was. She didn't know what had happened, so she couldn't imagine why I would call her and tell her this. I gave her the shortened version and told her that I had done the worst of the worst. I had been a namedropper and it had gotten me what I wanted ... twice in one day!

She consoled me as best as she could in the midst of teaching her class. As I began driving again, I remembered I was going to an event where I was the main speaker, to talk about Jesus and His love and having the characteristics of Christ. I wanted to turn around, go home, and bury my head in the desert. However, the ladies were all expecting me, and I had to proceed forward. I arrived without the bag of chips, with no explanation. I will admit that the evening went very well, but I said not a word to anyone about what I had done.

I was embarrassed and kind of felt that Jesus may have been a bit disappointed in me for the part I had played.

Driving home that evening after the event, I had my iPod on shuffle, and a song started playing by the Christian band called *Petra*. The song was *God Pleaser*. The song was basically talking about pleasing God or pleasing man, and if you choose to please God, then you will do what is right in His eyes. Really, God? Of the 1500 songs on my iPod this one just *happens* to come up as I'm struggling with my second police stop of the day?

I knew God was speaking to me, and as that song played, I asked God for forgiveness for my manipulation, my unethical bout of trying to bribe a police officer, and trying to work the situation for my own good. I then heard the Lord say very clearly to me, "When you go by that same spot where you were stopped, if the policeman are still there, I want you to go and pay for the ticket you should have gotten."

I couldn't argue or bribe my way out of this one because I knew I had a choice to be obedient or not. I told the Lord I would do as He asked. When I drove past the location, the men were not there, so I didn't pay the ticket that should have been mine. God knew the police officers would not be there, but I believe He was just trying to see if I would be obedient to Him or not. I really do want to be a God pleaser, but sometimes this crazy flesh of mine gets in the way. Do I drive slower now when I am rounding that corner? You better believe it! And I never carry chips up in the front seat with me. I don't want that temptation again.

Digging Deeper

1. First Samuel 15:22 (NLT) says, "But Samuel replied, 'What is more pleasing to the LORD: your burnt offerings and sacrifices or your obedience to his voice? Listen! Obedience is better than sacrifice, and submission is better than offering the fat of rams.'"

2. Sometimes we feel like we are doing great things for the Lord by sacrificing our time, our money, maybe a bag of chips, etc. What is it that God truly wants from us?

3. Have you ever heard that still small voice whisper for you to do something, and you chose not to do it because it would require too much or be too uncomfortable for you? Next time you hear the nudge of the Lord telling you to do something, act quickly and *make the choice of obedience.*

Chapter 14

Who Stole My Tube?

When we moved to Mexico, one of the hardest adjustments for me to make was when we received a bill, we had to actually go into the office and pay. I was used to putting a stamp on an envelope provided and sticking it in my mailbox or using the new, modern way of paying online. This strange, different way was going to be quite a change. Oftentimes, because of the mail system, we would not actually receive the bill but would need to go into the office on the due date, hopefully with enough money to pay the bill. After several years of doing this, I got pretty good at working my errands around places in the city I needed to go to pay my bills.

Usually, when we received the water and electric bills, I would clip them onto the refrigerator to remind me to pay them—an easy way of remembering. Here in Hermosillo, our water bill is under ten dollars a month, and all I needed to do with that bill was to walk a few yards to the neighborhood store to pay it. Much easier than trying to drive downtown in all of the traffic, find a parking spot, wait in line (sometimes for an hour), and then pay it.

One day, as Brian and I were returning home from teaching at the Bible institute, I got out of the passenger side of the car and noticed something different. Next to our driveway are the tubes for the city water. Anyone can walk by on the sidewalk and, if they choose, can play a joke on us by turning off the spigot. This results in cutting off the city water. It only has happened once, and it took us a long time to figure out why we didn't have water. On this particular day, I noticed the tube was missing. I couldn't believe it. I figured someone had stolen it, and we would have to go to Home Depot to replace our tube. Then Brian asked the question of all questions. "Did you pay the water bill?"

My reply came quickly. "Well of course I … *no*, I didn't!" I ran into the house to check the fridge, and sure enough, it was there—all trimmed in bright orange with the payment due date two weeks past. Oops! I saw it every day—even many times a day, as I opened that big beast for a snack or two, and I would always say, "*Mañana*—I'll just pay it mañana."

Well, mañana never came, and so I grabbed that bill *today* and walked as quickly as I could to our neighborhood store and paid it. The bill said $180 pesos, which I thought was strange since one month is only $90 pesos. I paid it and came back home. I was still wondering why in the world someone would steal our water tube and how that coincided with reminding me to actually pay my bill. I promptly got on the phone with the water company and apologized for not paying my bill and just casually told them that my tube had been stolen. I'm sure they laughed on the inside, though they were very professional-sounding in their voices. I was then informed that because I hadn't paid in two months, they took our tube.

Seriously, you took our tube? I thought to myself. I assured them I had just paid their bill, and they told me it would be one to three days before we got our tube back. Seriously, you took our tube? Who does that?

I got off the phone and had to break the hard news to my family. For a few days we were going to have to use the phrase, "If it's yellow, let it mellow." Flushing the toilet would use too much water from the tank on the roof, which only gets filled with the city water we wouldn't have for a few days. Once the water in the tank was gone, we would have no water. I didn't really know if three days meant three days or one week. Here in Mexico, they too often use the word *mañana.* Hey, where do you think I learned it?

I still couldn't believe someone actually physically drove to our house and took the tube for the water. They didn't flip a switch to cut off our city water; they just came and took the tube. Soon the tank was empty. We had to go outside to where the tube had been attached and turn on the spigot to fill our buckets with the city water. I felt like Laura Ingalls as we hauled buckets into the house, dumping some water into the toilet and leaving some for heating in order to wash.

After three days of no water (fortunately, we had to travel that weekend and were gone for two days), I called the office again early Monday morning and told them that the weekend had passed, and we still hadn't received our tube. They assured me by 4:00 p.m. it would be there. That time came and went, so I called again. They assured me by 8:00 p.m. it would be there. By 6:50 p.m. I was getting a little nervous that we would not have water for the night. My three children were at Tae Kwon Do; when they returned, well, they were going to stink—they needed to bathe. I told them before they left that when they got home, they might have to shower by getting their own water in our new Laura Ingalls style. They gave me the "Come on, Mom" attitude and went on to their class.

I got right back on that phone and called the office again, and they looked at their records and said, "Yes, we see that you've called three times today."

That's right, I had, and I spoke with them in Spanish too! They assured me the workers are out until 9:00 p.m., giving others back their tubes and that they would soon be at my house. I practically begged them in my American accent. I'm pretty sure they thought me needy. And at this point, I was just that.

Ten minutes later, there was a knock at my door, and it was like a miracle in the making for four days. The *Tube Man* was here. Yeah—what a glorious day! I was going to have water, and my kids weren't going to stink any longer.

I learned a fine lesson from all of this: pay your bills on time. Don't forget and don't leave them until mañana. Oh, and you'll be interested to know the reason my tube was so lovingly taken was because the month before, when I was traveling, I forgot to tell my husband to pay the bill. I guess if you miss two months here, know that your tube will be gone.

Now I know. I'm so good at procrastination, but this time it caught up with me and left me stinking.

Digging Deeper

1. Sometimes putting things off doesn't really seem to matter in the moment until you realize the consequences of not doing so when you should have. Proverbs 12:24 (ESV) says, "The hand of the diligent will rule, while the slothful will be put to forced labor."

2. Write down a time when you put off doing something, and later on it caused you to have to work harder.

3. Is there something you are putting off doing today for tomorrow that you know you should get to right away? Might as well get to it sooner rather than later.

Chapter 15

You Want Us to Pray with You?

In my younger years, I was a little bit of a stinker—not really a troublemaker, but let's say a *fun-maker*. The problem with teenagers who think they are fun-makers is that they often go a little too far in the name of fun and find themselves in a little bit of trouble. That's exactly where I found myself one time in my junior year of high school.

One of the highlights every year for me was attending our district church camp. I have very fond memories of the place because it was there, during a teen service, I asked Christ into my heart and promised to live for Him all the days of my life. It is there I made strong Christian friendships, found a boyfriend, and even had the opportunity years later to return as a pastor's wife.

That particular summer, I met up with my friends in the big dorm where we always stayed and bunked together in *our* section. It just so happened to be the section where the rowdy girls stayed—the fun-loving, happy-go-lucky, let's do some practical jokes kind of girls. The fun-makers. There was always a curfew at 11:00 p.m., when we all had to be in the dorms with lights out. This seemed to cramp our style a bit, so we began the week making plans to sneak out of the dorm and try to make it around the camp and back in the dorm without being caught. We had a goal: nothing illegal, nothing too delinquent, just an adventurous challenge.

To add some reassurance to the parents who sent their kids to this camp, the camp would hire pastors from around the district to stay up all night and act as security personnel. They would drive around the camp on their golf carts and do what security people do. This just added an element to our plan—to pass the night dodging security. They were always very thorough in making sure that everyone was where they should be. To keep the girls (like myself) from sneaking out the back way, they would lean a metal chair up against the door so that if it opened it would fall on the cement and make noise, thwarting any plan for escape. The chair became our first obstacle to surmount.

When the night came for our adventure, the six of us were ready. We put on our dark clothes, made our beds look as if there were bodies in them, and waited for our counselor to fall asleep. We never realized how much that hundred-year-old dorm creaked and cracked every time we took a step. As we proceeded down the back stairs quietly, we gently opened the door, fully aware of the chair behind it. And we moved it with success. As we opened the door, we quickly had to check for security personnel who might be sitting near the building (as they always did). As soon as they moved away from the building, we made our move, and we were home-free. We felt like giddy little schoolgirls but couldn't make a sound, for we would surely be heard.

We spent the next hour or so walking all around the camp, dodging security at all costs. It was invigorating, refreshing, intoxicating. We had sneaked out of the dorms at church camp—a story that would go down in the history books of the camp. We were something!

Around 2:00 a.m., we decided we needed a break—a place we could go where we wouldn't have to be on alert but could just relax. What better place to go than to the big auditorium where they held services every night. We were thrilled and a bit surprised to find that it was still unlocked. We figured it was unlocked in case adults wanted to go in early in the morning before the rest of the camp was awake. As we walked in and closed the doors, we began to laugh and brag that we had pulled the wool over everyone's eyes. Because we were now inside the building, we could make a bit of noise without fear of being caught.

As our eyes began to adjust to the darkness of the building, we saw movement of several people up near the altar. At two o'clock in the morning, it just wasn't possible. Or was it? As we approached the front, our worst nightmare for the early morning hours had come true. Unbeknownst to us, the counselors had planned earlier in the week to gather very early that morning for a prayer time in the auditorium. We had walked, or should I say, hooped and hollered into the end of their prayer time.

You can imagine the surprise they all showed as they saw six teenage girls (who were supposed to be sleeping) *attending* their prayer meeting without invitation. They began to laugh when they saw our wide eyes, realizing we'd been caught. Many things flashed through my mind at that point. Would I be sent home for disobeying the rules? Would I, the fun-maker, be disciplined for the whole camp to see? Would they find it funny and just let us go back to bed? (Okay, that one was pretty doubtful.)

The wisdom these counselors displayed was grand (probably from their time spent praying and not sneaking around all night). They invited us to pray with them. Pray with them? After all we'd been through, they wanted us to pray with them? We had no other choice but to do as they asked. Throughout the whole prayer time, each of us was wondering what would be our outcomes.

We were *sentenced* that evening for work during the following days at camp. We were to work in the field, where they were going to be putting a baseball diamond, and we were to pick up rocks. We were to clean the dining hall, and we were to clean the bathrooms. Not a bad punishment for disobeying the rules of the camp and acting contrary to what we knew to be right.

The worst part of the evening for me wasn't that we got caught or that we were disciplined. The worst part was the disappointment we saw on the faces of those counselors who trusted us. They'd had confidence that we were young ladies who would make good choices when we had the opportunity. There was no question that we had disobeyed and that we had disobeyed with joy and with flaunting of the rules.

It took me many years to realize there is a cost to disobedience. There wasn't much of a cost in picking up rocks in the mid-afternoon sun. The cost was the cost of giving up part of my character to a choice that was not pleasing to the Lord.

Digging Deeper

1. What does it mean to you to obey God? How do you feel when you disobey God?

2. I don't think the words of Jesus could be any more clear than they are in John 15:14 (ESV), "If you love me, you will keep my commandments."

3. Do you know what His commandments are? If you do not, commit to doing a word study on what obedience to God is. When you know what to do, then it makes it easier to make good, godly decisions and choices.

4. The hard part is when you know what is right and choose the opposite, as Paul says in his writings in Romans 7:14– 16 (The Message). "I can anticipate the response that is coming: 'I know that all God's commands are spiritual, but I'm not. Isn't this also your experience?' Yes. I'm full of myself—after all, I've spent a long time in sin's prison. What I don't understand about myself is that I decide one way, but then I act another, doing things I absolutely despise. So if I can't be trusted to figure out what is best for myself and then do it, it becomes obvious that God's command is necessary."

Chapter 16

Worst Mother in the World

It was a wonderful, sunny, summer's day. Our family lived out in the country in Michigan, in the middle of literally thousands of acres of cornfields. It was an amazing place to live. Across the street were the grain elevators owned by the people who rented us our house. There were continuous tractors going in and out of the farm. In fact, when most children say *Ma-ma* or *Da-da* first, our little guy said *tractor*. Every day he would watch the many different kinds of tractors outside the window with joy and enthusiasm. So no surprise what his first word was.

My son Mitchell, the tractor enthusiast, was twenty-one months old when Zachary was born six weeks earlier. Brian was on a mission trip for ten days—the first time I'd really been alone for much time with two children. To pass the time together we would often take the two dogs outside and head for the sandbox. On this particular day, we were doing the normal sandbox adventures, and Zachary was strapped in his *bucket* (car seat that doubles as a carrier) under the shade tree, and of course, the dogs were frolicking around in the green grass, chasing butterflies, each other, and their own tails. It was a perfect day—one of those days where all is right with the world—and you just feel content. And then we saw it: the biggest John Deere tractor we had ever seen so close to us, plowing in the field right on the edge of our lawn.

Upon doing a double-take, I realized it was one of the big combines. I mean, that thing was huge. Mitchell's eyes got big, and he could hardly contain his excitement. It was right there in front of us. Suddenly it stopped, and Mitchell, frozen in position, watched the man as he got out and walked over to us. He asked me if we would like to go on a ride as he did his next row down the field. A dream of a lifetime for my boy, this couldn't be missed. With excitement myself, I said to him, "Give me a second to put the dogs in their pen, and we'll be ready to go." I told Mitchell what was going to be happening, and he just was one big smile.

I locked the dogs in the pen, scooped up Mitchell, and climbed into that big combine. With excitement, we started our journey, and Mitchell watched and listened as the combine did its work and turned to the next row. He laughed and was even more thrilled when the farmer offered him a peppermint candy. He just sat on my lap and enjoyed life. I chatted with the farmer, thanking him for being so thoughtful as to stop and offer us a ride and how Mitchell would be talking about it for a long time (Mitchell was already talking a lot at this point).

Suddenly, I felt a sickness inside. We were ten minutes into the ride, and my heart literally almost stopped. "Oh, my goodness, I left my newborn baby under the tree!" I exclaimed.

Inside I was frantic but tried to play it cool on the outside. I was finding it hard to contain my emotions as I realized I had forgotten I had another child. What kind of mother forgets she has two children? My dear, sweet Zachary was lying in his bucket under the tree, sound asleep when I left him but was probably in fear now that Mommy had *abandoned* him! I was horrified. And now that I had admitted it out loud, I was sure the farmer was going to call social services on me, and Zachary would be taken away before Brian even returned home. What was I going to do?

"Stop, please. I need to get out and run back to my baby."

His reply was slow, but it sunk in in one of those awful ways. He said, "I'm sorry, ma'am, but it will take longer for you to run back than it will for us to keep going in this row and turn around and head back, for we are three-quarters of a mile away."

I thought, *What? I left my baby and went that far away? Are you kidding me? I have to sit here calmly and wait for him to finish this row and turn around?* Trying to keep my cool so as not to scare Mitchell (who had no idea of the problem and was enjoying the ride thoroughly), I told the farmer to continue on. Those next fifteen minutes were the longest fifteen minutes of my life. I envisioned the other farm hands finding Zachary, knocking on the house door, and with no response, taking Zach to someone who would care for him properly. I pictured someone just going along for a nice summer drive and seeing my baby under the tree and taking him to raise themselves (since obviously, his own mother hadn't remembered he had been born!).

Then I realized I would have to tell Brian what I had done. Oh, the sickness in the pit of my stomach in having to tell my husband that, after several hours of labor and him helping me for the last six weeks, I literally had forgotten we had another child, and he was going to be growing up *in the system* with new parents. Now the ironic part about all of this is that I told the farmer to wait a second because I had to put my dogs in their pen. Not that I had to grab my baby in the bucket to bring along with us, but I had to make sure the *dogs* were secure! I had to be the worst mother who had ever lived on the earth.

As we pulled closer to the barn, our yard began to come into view. I still was unable to see the tree Zachary was supposed to be under, but I was chomping at the bit with anticipation as it came into view. When he stopped the combine, I smiled very kindly (trying not to throw up), thanked him, pretty much yanked Mitchell out of the tractor, and sprinted across the yard, where I was sure Zachary would be gone from his bucket or crying his head off, scarred for life.

We arrived at the tree, and I set Mitchell down. When I looked down into the bucket, my newborn, Zach, was lying there sleeping as I had left him—not a care in the world and no idea I had been gone. No idea that I was the worst mother in the world, he was enjoying the breeze of the day. I grabbed hold of the handles of the bucket, took Mitchell's hand, and went inside as the tears and anxiety started welling up inside me. I put Zachary down in the living room (still asleep) and took Mitchell up to his room, telling him he needed to spend some down time in there while Mommy did a few things. Mitchell, being the good boy that he was and probably still in awe of his tractor adventure, did what he was told and stayed in his room. I kissed his head and went downstairs.

And then I lost it. I lost it like never before. I cried, I wailed, I stomped, and I took my sleeping son out of the bucket and held him as if I would never let go. I cried tears that soaked his outfit, and I just loved on him, telling him how sorry I was for forgetting him. I reassured him that he was important to me but that Mommy, well, Mommy had just not gotten used to having two children.

Oh, the pain I was enduring was like no other. I thanked God for keeping my child safe under the tree, I thanked God that no one had stolen him, and I thanked God that social services hadn't come to my door ... yet. Oh, no, I still had to worry about that. The farmer was going to turn me in, I just knew it. I called my mother, who lived five miles away, and told her about what had happened and how unfit I was. She tried to calm me and offered to come over. My freaking out episode was pretty much over, and I was thinking fairly clear-headed, so I thought I would be okay. And then I said, "Mom, what if people come and take him away from me? I didn't mean to forget him. I love him. How will I ever explain this to Brian? If they do come for him, when do you think it will be?"

I had never been as thankful for my mom as I was in that moment when she reassured me that everything was going to be all right and that she doubted anyone was going to take Zachary away. Zachary is now nineteen, just starting his second year of college. No one ever came and investigated my horrible mother-ness, and I never forgot him like that again. When Brian arrived home, I told him what had happened; he just encouraged me by saying as a new mom, things are hard, and sometimes things happen.

I vowed *never* to tell anyone what had happened. But then, several years later, as I began speaking to women and moms with young children, I realized I surely couldn't be the only one who had done something like that. Could I? So I began integrating that story into my talks, realizing if I was the only one, they would think I was rotten and move on. But if I wasn't, they might not feel so alone in their experiences. It was amazing how many women would come up to me after my talks and tell me their stories about leaving their children behind. I somehow felt a part of this secret club of mothers who thought they were horrible but really weren't. I realized we make mistakes in this life and can either die inside (always focusing on that mistake) or move on. I chose to move on—not in a John Deere combine, but just move on in life, away from my new-mother error.

Digging Deeper

1. Have you ever made a whopper of a mistake (or, as in my case, many whoppers of mistakes)? How did it make you feel?

2. Read these Scripture verses, which are meant to remind you that you are not alone in your mistakes.

    Psalm 37:24 (NLT) says, "Though they stumble, they will never fall, for the LORD holds them by the hand."

    Isaiah 41:10 (NLT) says, "Don't be afraid, for I am with you. Don't be discouraged, for I am your God. I will strengthen you and help you. I will hold you up with my victorious right hand."

    Psalm 91:4 (NLT) says, "He will cover you with his feathers. He will shelter you with his wings. His faithful promises are your armor and protection."

3. So what can we do after we've made a big blunder?

    Philippians 3:13 (NIV) says, "Brothers and sisters, I do not consider myself yet to have taken hold of it. But one thing I do: Forgetting what is behind and straining toward what is ahead."

    Hebrews 12:1 (NIV) says, "Therefore, since we are surrounded by such a huge crowd of witnesses to the life of faith, let us strip off every weight that slows us down, especially the sin that so easily trips us up. And let us run with endurance the race God has set before us."

4. Sometimes it's difficult for us to forget the mistake we have made and move on. Pray right now for God to help you put behind you the things that need to be put behind and to give you the strength to move forward from your mistakes.

Chapter 17

Punctured Pride

My husband always shakes his head at me when I come up with some *great* idea of how to make our lives easier. He has been with me long enough to know my ideas about making our lives easier are really code for "this is going to be a crazy amount of work."

I suppose our moving a hundred-year-old small barn wasn't any different. We had horses and needed an out building for their hay and gear. On a pastor's salary you can't just call someone and have him or her build a thing of that size without saving for years. When our friends said they were getting rid of their very old barn and offered it to us if we disassembled it and transferred it to our house, I was thrilled. It would have the charm of an older building, I'd paint it red and it was *free*. Bonus!

I told my husband all about this great adventure we would take together. It would be fun. Fun wasn't the word that came to his mind. *She really doesn't know what she's getting herself into*, he thought. In hindsight, he was so very right.

We went over on a sunny, summer afternoon and began taking this outbuilding apart. We were careful not to mar any of the wood, as we would be rebuilding it on our property. It was really hard work. Just getting the roof off about did me in. Of course my husband looked at me with an expression in his eyes that said, *Still having that fun you talked so much about?*

Oh, it wouldn't take long; we could do this, was my thought. And we did. It took several days to tear it down, load it into our little Dodge Dakota, and take it six miles to our house. We worked diligently and could see ourselves close to being done.

One of the very last loads consisted of the really heavy things. We had already taken long boards and stacked them up near the horse fence, but these were going to be a little more awkward to carry. They were the sliding barn doors, and they were very big. We backed up as close as we could to where we were going to put the oversized doors on the ground. We each had to get on one side of the truck bed and pick up the door, as if we were carrying a casket. Once we got to the end of the truck, we would turn the door, and I would walk backward just a few feet to where we would set it down. I was a strong gal, so it didn't seem that hard of a task (and for most people, it really wouldn't be).

One step backward, two steps backward. Though I had a good grip and balance on the door, my foot hit something. I started to sway from side to side, only to fall straight down, as if I was awkwardly trying to sit on the ground. There was no way to stop the fall because I had the barn door in my hand. So I just had to let gravity take over. I was really hoping to fall on the soft green grass, which might only put a little grass stain on my good shorts. I never imagined what would happen next.

When I hit, I hit hard, and I did not hit the ground. I happened to hit one of the long boards we had stacked there earlier, and this long board just so happened to have a giant, king-sized, humongous, rusty nail sticking straight out of it. Oh, yes, you guessed correctly. The nail went right into my left butt cheek. If you are looking for a more medically correct way to say it, you might say that the nail arrived deep inside the left side of the buttocks or gluteus maximus. However, as you may be focusing on the correct lingo, all I know is that, at that moment, I had gotten poked in the butt and it hurt. My first reaction was to jump up.

Now I don't want to get too graphic, but when one jumps up quickly after getting a nail in the buttocks, one does not rise from the same angle that one fell, thus causing a bit more of the ouch factor. The hundred-year-old rusty nail went in about an inch and came out, leaving just a puncture. Not only a puncture in my skin, but a puncture in my good shorts and my underclothes. I had just been punctured by a nasty, bacteria-ridden piece of steel. I stood there—shocked. My husband stood there, wide-eyed in shock as well.

He got into the "Okay, Laurie has been hurt again" mode and said that we should probably go into the bathroom and clean out the puncture to prevent infection. We walked into the house, as I grumbled the whole way about how things always happen to me, and who gets a nail in their butt?

Seriously, who does that? Brian, in his sweet gentleness, lips still pressed, would respond, "Only you, honey, only you."

We tried to clean it out, but honestly, how do you clean out a one-inch puncture wound? You can pour peroxide on it, but it will only go in so far. For fifteen minutes, he tried to clean it, and then he finally said, "I can take this no longer. May I please laugh? It's killing me to hold it in."

Let me explain a little. You see, it wasn't funny to him in the sense that I was hurt, but because I *always* hurt myself. The urge to laugh came from the fact that "this was a new one for Laurie." Who would have ever guessed falling on her butt onto a rusty nail? Understanding his request, I said he could laugh, and laugh he did. Then the fact that I might truly be hurt kicked in for him, and he said the dreaded words, "I think you are going to have to go to the hospital and get it cleaned out so that you don't get an infection.

"Oh, no, no, no, no!" I couldn't go to the hospital here in our small town. I knew people who worked in the emergency room. A guy from our church worked there. A guy! He was always there, and I knew he would be there that afternoon. No way was I going to grace the hospital with my rusty, punctured pride, knowing that he could be there. I refused. I would rather have lost my butt cheek to amputation than humiliate myself by having this man do the checking.

Hmm, amputation of the butt cheek. That wasn't a bad idea. I really could have used a bit of that, and if they could give me a two-for-one maybe I would go to the hospital. *No.* That's the rust and infection inside my body talking. I would not go! That day, my friends and family got a good laugh out of my woes, and my kids even laughed a little at their silly mom, who always does something weird to hurt herself. Life went on like it normally does. I think I even finished unloading the wood but just a little more carefully this time.

The following day, my husband sat down with me and, in all seriousness, told me I really should go get the wound checked out by a doctor because it was getting red around the area of the puncture. Oh, give me strength! I made the decision to call the nurse practitioner in town to whom I had gone before. She was a female and *didn't* go to my church.

I made the phone call, and a secretary answered. I told her I needed to get in that day to see the nurse practitioner. Then the awkward, necessary question came. "What is this pertaining?"

I could lie. Yes, I will lie. No, I can't. I'm a pastor's wife, I love Jesus, and I don't want to lie. I could plead the fifth, but that would make me sound rude. Oh, just tell her. "Well, I need to see her because yesterday I sat on a nail, and it went about an inch into my butt. I'm afraid it is going to get infected."

I have to give her credit; she didn't laugh or ask if I was joking. She was very professional and got me in quickly. I had to give her my name and my birth date. I think giving her my name was just so that, when she hung up, she could gather the office staff around to tell them who was coming in soon and why. Oh, bother. So I went.

When I walked into the office, I just knew everyone behind the glass was stifling chuckles. They walked me through to the examination room, and I waited and waited. When the nurse practitioner arrived, I had to tell my story and my embarrassment about having to come in (knowing that I needed to) and probably a bunch of other babble she really didn't care about. She was a professional and was there to see my butt cheek, that's all.

So I felt degraded but had to take off my pants (new shorts, without a hole in them) and bend over the table so she could get a good view—humiliation at its highest level. Well, probably not, but it felt like it just then. I wasn't in danger of amputation, but she gave me an antibiotic and told me it would be cleared up in a few days. The only thing that's left behind is the mark on the left behind.

Digging Deeper

1. I sure was embarrassed to tell anyone, especially anyone at the hospital, I had sat on a nail. Do you realize that sin is the same way? We fall into sin over and over and know that we need help but are too embarrassed to tell someone and ask for help. It's a humbling experience to admit to someone something we have done wrong. What does James 5:16 (NIV) tell us to do with our sins? "Therefore confess your sins to each other and pray for each other so that you may be healed. The prayer of a righteous person is powerful and effective."

2. Pride is the opposite of humility. Pride is the sin that will keep us from being humble. What does the Bible say about pride?

Proverbs 16:18 (MSG) says, "First pride, then the crash—the bigger the ego, the harder the fall."

Proverbs 29:23 (NLT) says, "Pride ends in humiliation, while humility brings honor."

3. God desires a humble heart. Read these scriptures about humility. Colossians 3:12 (NIV) says, "Therefore, as God's chosen people, holy and dearly loved, clothe yourselves with compassion, kindness, humility, gentleness and patience."

   James 4:10 (NIV) says, "Humble yourselves before the Lord, and he will lift you up."

   Proverbs 22:4 (NLT) says, "True humility and fear of the LORD lead to riches, honor, and long life."

   Proverbs 22:4 (NLT) says, "True humility and fear of the LORD lead to riches, honor, and long life."

4. Is there a sin in your life today you need to humble yourself about and share with someone else to help get the proper healing you need? Don't put it off. Go do it!

Chapter 18

The Overly-Friendly, New Lady in Town

Every few years, we have to return to Michigan from the mission field to share in different churches what God has been doing in the country we serve. We had bought a house in our small community in Michigan two years before returning and were so excited to be able to live in it for our year home. While away, we had people check in on the house and hired a lawn service to mow the lawn. How fun to return and do all of this ourselves. Everything was new and exciting for us, and I wasn't afraid to show people just how happy I was ... sometimes in a very friendly way.

We were looking forward to living in what we knew would be a quiet neighborhood. Across the street was a medical care facility for older folks. Next door was a retired school teacher, and on the other side was an adult care home for people who were unable to continue living by themselves.

One day, I happened to look next door, only to see a friend, Paul, who, several years before had been in the Sunday school class I had taught. He was moving his mother into the facility. I didn't get a chance to say hello to him but hoped I would at some point. The joy of living in a small town for me is, knowing people when I go to the store or walk down the sidewalk or look across the yard. (It is not a joy, however, if you have to go to the emergency room, as noted in the previous story.) After living for several years in a city of a million people, I was looking forward to being back in this small-town atmosphere.

Just a few days after we moved in, there was a knock at the door. We were all busy unpacking boxes and trying to get the house in some sort of order. The excitement of being in our home was still with us, and we were just all-around happy. As I went to the door to answer it, I saw Paul (the man who had been moving his mom in next door) standing there. It had been a few years since I'd seen him, so I thought, as I walked through the porch to get the door, that he looked a bit older, had lost a little more hair, and had gained some weight. But, well, haven't we all?

I opened the door, and in true Mexican greeting style, I wrapped my arms around him, hugged him tightly, and said with much joy and enthusiasm, "Hi, how are you doing? It is *so* good to see you."

He kind of did the awkward pat on the back as we hugged, and when I pulled back, he smiled and said with not as much enthusiasm, "I'm well. Thank you."

I thought to myself that he would be a little more excited to see me after so many years, but then, I had been in Mexico for the past five years where, in greeting others, everyone hugs and kisses. It's a very warm culture. I remembered that sometimes people in the United States aren't as anxious to hug as I am. Not a big deal.

And then it happened—the start of my heart dropping and thudding on the floor. He reached his hand out to me to give me a piece of paper and said, "Well, here is the bill for your lawn service." Ah, no, no, no, it couldn't be. Was this *not* Paul? Are you even kidding me?

This was *not* Paul. This was the lawn guy, whom I had *never* met. Did I say whom I'd *never* met? Oh, mercy! How was I to get out of this one? I mean, Paul and I weren't good friends, and I know people change but to make that kind of mistake, really? I began to backpedal out of our conversation, still trying to be upbeat, as if I greeted everyone like that. You know, trying to cover it all up so that, in his mind, it was really all good.

We ended our exchange, and I knew he thought that I had been the over-friendly missionary who had probably been in the mountains of Mexico with no interaction for too long and that the site of the lawn guy (or any person, for that matter) prompted the need in me to hug tightly.

I was just imagining his thoughts as he walked away. *Wow, she's a friendly gal. I wonder if I should come back tomorrow? Tee-hee. Her poor husband. I wonder if they sent her back home from the mission field because she was crazy?*

I closed the door and walked through the porch back into the house to my family. My husband, Brian, asked (as anyone would after a knock on the door), "Who was at the door?"

It was a simple question that normally would require a simple answer such as, "It was the lawn guy giving us the bill." Wouldn't that have been an easy answer to give? But it just wasn't that easy because I was beet-red and beginning to laugh hysterically. Brian, with reason, wondered how a simple knock at the door could make me laugh so hard. I proceeded to tell him what I had done. He laughed and said, "So I'll make sure that I come and get you when he returns tomorrow?"

"Very funny," I replied. Now there is a benefit to living in a city of a million people. You rarely see someone twice after you have done something embarrassing. But because I love living in a small town, I knew I wouldn't be so lucky. In fact, for the rest of the summer, I saw the lawn guy at least once a week as he mowed the lawns of the neighbors on either side of us. I never ran up and hugged him again but just gave a smile and a wave. I can't help but wonder if he was disappointed that he never got another hug or if he was relieved. Maybe next time, I'll just shake his hand and thank him for the bill.

Digging Deeper

1. The 1828 edition of the *Noah Webster Dictionary* defines hospitality as generous and friendly treatment of visitors and guests. It was evident by the hug I gave the lawn man that I was being very hospitable.[3]

On a scale from one to ten, how hospitable are you when someone comes to your home?
    1(not very) 2 3 4 5 6 7 8 9 10 (very)

2. The original Greek word for *hospitality* is *philoxenos*, which means, "love of strangers." The Greek word *philoneksía*, by combining *phílos* or friend and *xenos*, or stranger, basically means friendliness or generosity given, whether it's along the fence post in your yard or having someone into your home. What are some ways this month you can intentionally show hospitality to your friends and neighbors or maybe even to someone you don't yet know? Write down two ways, and then work the plan.

   a.

   b.

3. Throughout the New Testament is verse after verse about people being welcoming and hospitable to Jesus, Paul, and many other Christ-followers. Matthew 8:20 (NIV) says, "Jesus replied, 'Foxes have dens and birds have nests, but the Son of Man has no place to lay his head.'" What does this tell you about Jesus?

4. Can you imagine always "being on the road" and having to rely on others to care for your needs? Read these verses about those who took care of Jesus. Mark 2:15 (NIV) says, "While Jesus was having dinner at Levi's house, many tax collectors and sinners were eating with him and his disciples, for there were many who followed him."

Mark 1:29 (NIV) says, "As soon as they left the synagogue, they went with James and John to the home of Simon and Andrew."

Luke 7:36 (NIV) says, "When one of the Pharisees invited Jesus to have dinner with him, he went to the Pharisee's house and reclined at the table."

Luke 10:38 (NIV) says, "As Jesus and his disciples were on their way, he came to a village where a woman named Martha opened her home to him."

5. Luke 9:1–5 (NLT) says:

> One day Jesus called together his twelve disciples and gave them power and authority to cast out all demons and to heal all diseases. Then he sent them out to tell everyone about the Kingdom of God and to heal the sick. 'Take nothing for your journey,' he instructed them. 'Don't take a walking stick, a traveler's bag, food, money, or even a change of clothes. Wherever you go, stay in the same house until you leave town. And if a town refuses to welcome you, shake its dust from your feet as you leave to show that you have abandoned those people to their fate.'" When Jesus sent out the twelve disciples, He was very clear in telling them how to deal with those who didn't show them hospitality.

Chapter 19

Confessions of an Airline Snob

I really despise flying. I didn't used to despise it. In fact, it was just the opposite. When I was younger, I'd get that feeling of excitement and joy of the anticipation of it all. I never flew on an airplane as a child. My first flight was when I went to Florida for spring training with my college softball team. I even received a free pair of wings to signify I had flown. I remember walking down the ramp to board the plane, feeling like I was the coolest person in the world. Before the return flight, I was so excited to have flown to Florida that I hugged a palm tree outside of the airport, not knowing that I would be bringing new *friends* with me on the flight.

About the time I sat in my seat, my legs began to itch. The friends I had carried on were red ants from the palm tree. I couldn't slap them off my legs fast enough. But even with my legs itching terribly, I still felt like I was something special, just being able to fly.

That was then; this is now. Now, although I am thankful for the speed to get from one place to the other, I am all done with the "Wow, look at me; I'm cool for flying" moments. If

I am totally honest, I'm almost bothered by having to jump through all of the hoops to fly.

Here I sit this evening, writing my story on a second-, third-, no, maybe fourth-rate airline. My husband told me not to book this airline, even though it appeared to be cheaper. He was very clear that, from his experience, it was not worth it. Always wanting to save a buck, I figured it couldn't be *that* bad. So now I sit on this horrible flight, all because it didn't cost us as much. Oh, it's cheap, alright. I feel like I'm riding in a moving Petri dish, complete with every germ possible on this earth. I breathe in and feel as if I'll be sick. I overhear my travel companions joking about traveling in a flying urinal. Gross, right? I guess I can't blame them for saying this because we walked on the plane, only to be greeted by the strong smell of urine and a dirty baby diaper. I bet if there was a first class on this plane (which there totally isn't) we might be smelling fresh flowers or something pleasant. But we will never know because I chose the fourth-rate airline.

I guess my mission supporters back in the United States would be happy that I was being a good steward of the money we receive. But honestly, next time I think they would want me to pick the second- or third-rate flight, where maybe the smell of baby diapers is a little fresher.

Wearing headphones on the flight and listening to soothing music is not a bad idea, because when having these on, you can't hear the sounds all around. Sounds like the child screaming bloody murder, even though he's old enough to know better, the lady behind me sneezing, the college student in front of me blowing his nose (making it very obvious he had a lot in there), or the man sitting across from me coughing. I've never really been a germophobe, but when I am on an airplane my senses heighten, and I feel very dirty. I want to wash my hands, but that would mean going into the smelly bathroom. I want to put my comfy, crescent-shaped pillow behind my head, but I don't really want it to touch the seat. I, at least, will put my head against the seat, while my daughter will spend the next two hours sitting up straight, refusing for her back, arms, or hair to touch the back of her seat.

And we don't want to forget about the garbage left behind from the last flight. Under the seat in front of us is a used plastic medicine dispenser and, of course, my daughter just had to point out to me the chewed gum stuck to the seat in front of her. I almost can't contain the shivers going through my body at this moment.

I recall flying nineteen hours to the Philippines and sitting in a row of five seats. My seat did not recline, and my husband's seat was broken. We aren't the smallest people, and so fitting in the seats was hard enough. But to have to eat our knees the whole way was a challenge. At least to keep us occupied for the long flight they had in-flight movies. As luck would have it, I happened to get stuck behind a big-headed man who blocked my chance of any view of the movie. I just figured I'd readjust, but every time I did, he readjusted as well. It was like synchronized restlessness. Wait a minute. Is that throw-up I smell? Oh, please say no!

When I fly by myself, I try to say hello to the people around me and can kind of get a feel if they want to talk or not. Honestly, sometimes I am just so whipped that I put my headphones on and tune everyone out. One particular flight I got on I happened to be sitting by a twenty-something guy. I was in my early twenties myself, and so we began to chitchat. He seemed nice, and then he said, "So do you believe in UFOs and aliens?"

Really? I just met you; can't we talk about normal things? I thought.

He went on to explain his whole philosophy of why they both existed and what he had seen. I just smiled and thought to myself, *Can't Milwaukee be closer, please?*

When my son Zachary was just three weeks old, I flew alone with him to Denver. Oh, I know what some of you will say: "Taking that sweet little boy on an airplane so young—what a crime. His poor ears!" Well, no worries because his ears were fine, and the flight itself was pretty uneventful until I got off with my baby and my bag and realized I had to go to the bathroom. Hmm, how does one do this with a newborn? No way would I ask a stranger to hold him, for who knew where he would end up? I wasn't going to let him out of my sight. That meant one thing: bag and baby into the bathroom stall. For some reason the handicap stall was not available, so I had to cram the bag in there and balance, yes, balance, my three-week-old baby in my arms as I undid my pants, did what I came to do, and pulled my pants back up. Talk about out of breath. Phew! But I had done it and hadn't dropped my boy. Point for mom!

So back to sitting here on the fourth-rate airline, it just got bumped to a fifth-rate airline. Why, you might ask? I have been watching the stewardesses coming with their cart, anticipating a cold Diet Coke and a little bag of flight cookies. I just found out that if I want those items I have to pay more than two dollars. Will. Not. Do. It.

I can't leave you all thinking that I complain about every one of my flights because that just would not be true. I remember the flight when I got to go into the cockpit and talk to the pilot (pre-9/11). I remember going right up to where the passengers got off the plane, hugging my loved one, and not having to wait behind the designated line (also pre-9/11).

There was also the flight I took from Costa Rica to Florida. I'd had surgery four days before because I had shredded my Achilles tendon. For my birthday my girlfriends from Michigan had paid my way to meet them in Ft. Lauderdale for a long girl's weekend. We were so excited about being together again. When I ended up having major surgery, I told my doctor afterward of my plans, just to make sure I'd be out of the hospital in time to catch my flight. He told me my surgeon may not let me go. I began to beg him to plea-e-e-a-a-ase tell the surgeon how important it was to me. Finally, it was decided (by the grace of God) I could go. Yep, I was surprised too. The doctors cut slightly into my cast in case I had to rip it off on the plane because of the pressure.

I got out of the hospital one day before my flight left, got my wheelchair in order, and packed my bags. What I remember most about my flight were the two people I sat next to. They were flying home from a mission's trip. We began talking, and I told them I was a missionary. We shared some neat stories, and then we landed. The airline workers brought the wheelchair to the plane door for me to hop to. The most awesome God-thing happened. This couple, that I had been talking to the whole flight, stood up and said, "We know you are traveling alone, so we want to walk with you (more like, they walk, I roll) until you see your friends."

What a blessing! This couple rolled me through immigration and to baggage claim until we heard singing and birthday horns coming from a crowd. That would be my friends and all of the strangers around whom they got to volunteer to give me my birthday welcome to the states. This couple hugged me and sent me on my way. I don't remember their names or even what they looked like, but I do remember that, on a day I thought my airline experience was going to be harder than ever, God provided me with just what I needed.

So today I may be a little grossed out by all I'm taking in—the sounds, the smells, etc., but sometimes it's just a matter of perspective. Perhaps for someone today, anxious to get home to a loved one, this will be his or her best flight ever. Maybe for someone else this is their first flight, and he or she is filled with emotion and the sense of feeling really important, just as I had so many years ago. I guess I will just lean my seat back and enjoy the ride despite the sounds and the smells. It could always be worse; there could be chickens and goats on the flight.

Digging Deeper

1. Do you ever feel you deserve better than what you are getting at the time? Why do you feel that way?

2. I've had to deal with selfishness my whole life and try to keep it in check. I recall at one time seeing a T-shirt that said, "It's all about me" and wanting to buy it to wear. The Bible says in Philippians 2:3 (NLT), "Don't be selfish; don't try to impress others. Be humble, thinking of others as better than yourselves."

    a. That's pretty specific, isn't it? List in what ways you are selfish.
    b. List some ways you can practice being humble this week

3. Remember the verse in Romans 12:3 (NLT) that says, "Because of the privilege and authority God has given me, I give each of you this warning: Don't think you are better than you really are. Be honest in your evaluation of yourselves, measuring yourselves by the faith God has given us."

    In other words, don't go out and buy the T-shirt that says, "It's all about me" because it really isn't.

Chapter 20

A Little More than a Tree Hugger

When I was forty, our family had the privilege of living in Costa Rica for eight months to attend language school. It was one of the hardest times of my life but also a time when we had many adventures and made great memories.

The school was always good about planning weekend trips for the students so that they could truly see the culture and the life of this beautiful Central American country. We realized we might never be back in this country again, so we tried to save our money to be able to go on some of these trips.

One weekend, we went and stayed at a resort at the base of one of the famous active volcanoes. While we were there, one of the options was to pay extra to zip-line over the rainforest. This was a dream but something with a family of five we could not afford. A dear friend took Brian aside and told him he and his family would like to pay for us to go zip-lining with them. We were very humbled by their offer and, with joy, accepted it.

I was thrilled as I watched my children put on all of their gear and felt along with them their emotion about this scary but exciting adventure we were about to spend the next two hours having. We drove to the top of the mountain where we would begin the fourteen stations that were going to get us down on our zip-lines. It proved to be an incredible journey, with views that couldn't be explained other than to say they were examples of the majesty of God.

After about station ten, we became more and more confident with what we were doing and had the option of going upside down in Spiderman form (which my son Mitchell decided to do) or fly like Superman (which I opted to do). I was flying over the tops of the trees in the Costa Rican rainforest. Who gets to do that? I was in heaven. As I soared over the green canvas, I felt the peace and tranquility of God. It was a surreal moment for me—one I will never forget.

When we came to station fourteen, I had another moment I will never forget. I would have to say this moment was the total opposite of the peace and tranquility I felt only one station before. Most of the children were sent down on the last run, ahead of the adults. As I stood on the tree stand waiting for my turn, I heard communication on the guide's walkie-talkie that one of the kids had been hurt on the way down. Because of my minimal Spanish at the time, I didn't get the whole story—just bits and pieces. My mother's heart kicked in, and I was afraid it was one my children and was lamenting that I wasn't there to help my child.

It was finally my turn to go down (the wait seemed like forever after I heard the communication). The guide told me very clearly this was a very fast run, and I would need to start braking about the time I left the tree stand. I told him I understood and proceeded to go down the last cable of this amazing adventure above the treetops. Just after I took off, I saw a number of people in the green grass below gathered around a child. All I could do was look down and try to see who the child was. When I looked up, all I could see on the final stand (where I was to land) was the guide with a frantic look on his face. His arms were moving up and his mouth was saying *"Alto!"* ("Stop!")

Things happened very quickly after that. I remember going in way too fast, with one foot hitting the guide in the ribs and the other foot hitting the tree. Ouch! I learned a couple of things later I hadn't been aware of. One was that I had hit so hard it actually flipped me upside down (something I didn't realize or remember). Also, a friend of ours who was an ER doctor was sitting down below with my husband, Brian, and told him as he saw me coming in too fast, "She is about to break both of her legs."

I was stunned, to say the least. Would you believe there were no visible injuries? I felt this was a gift from God. There is no doubt my head rattled around for a few days, but I was alright. People were just amazed, and my family and I were thankful, by the grace of God, I hadn't broken either or both of my legs or sustained any visible injuries.

I did feel badly for plowing into the guide at forty mph (with all of the weight that this big gal carries). The next day, I saw him up on one of the tree stands and asked how he was. He gave me a thumbs-up, and I was so relieved. My friend later told me this poor guy had gone to the hospital; I had hurt his ribs so badly he had terrible bruises. I guess that day we both went home with a souvenir of our time spent together with the group in our treetop adventure. He had bruised ribs, and I had the memory of an incredible day with a big tree that, somehow, in a very quick manner, just happened to grow up in front of me.

Digging Deeper

1. Name a time when you forgot or just didn't listen, and there was a consequence.

2. John 10:27 (NASB) says, "My sheep hear My voice, and I know them, and they follow Me. If the sheep aren't listening to their master, I get this picture in my mind that they are all over the pasture and the shepherd is scrambling around trying to gather them."

3. In the verse above, what happens when the sheep actually listen to the shepherd's voice?

4. In this passage Jesus is talking about Himself as the shepherd and us being the sheep. Are you a sheep who listens to the instructions and can easily follow because you know the sound of His voice? Or are you the distracted sheep that may or may not listen, depending on your situation at the time?

5. What are the benefits of being the person who knows the voice of Jesus and hears what He says? What are the negative consequences of not listening to Jesus?

Chapter 21

I Almost Killed the Pastor's Wife

For six years in small-town Michigan, we were fortunate enough to be on staff at a church with my husband's sister, Kristy. Her husband was the senior pastor, and he brought Brian on staff as a youth and worship pastor. While we were there, it was a lot of fun—more fun than I could ever have imagined.

We lived down the lane from each other on the church property, so oftentimes, we would wave back and forth if I was out back on my deck and my sister-in-law was working in her flowerbeds. It was just a dream-come-true kind of situation. Kristy and I were very close, making it easy for us to do things together. She is one of those people whom Anne of Green Gables would call a "kindred spirit."

If you knew Kristy long enough, you began to realize below that sweet, kind, loving exterior was a stinker. She loved to play pranks, and she loved to make it look like someone else did them. Her sarcasm was well beyond that of the normal person, almost as if she practiced it often (and she did). Our families were a wonderful combination together, not only in ministry but in friendship as well.

Kristy was also the Christian education director for the church, so she had office hours at the same time as my husband, her little brother, Brian. Sometimes she would become bored, and then her mind would begin scheming. Honestly, it was always fun to hear what silly thing she did to one of her coworkers.

The first week Brian was there at the church, he had his office all put together nicely so that the next day he could go in and begin his work. When he arrived at his office, his office chair had disappeared. Thinking that maybe someone had moved it into the conference room, he looked in there and, with no luck finding it, extended the search to the rest of the church. The chair was nowhere to be found. How strange. Finally, after much time had passed that day, the secretary came out of the women's bathroom and asked the staff (Kristy included), "Why is there an office chair in the handicap stall of the women's bathroom?"

Brian knew right then and there he was going to have to keep a close eye on that older sister of his, for she was going to be trouble. I don't know if she ever admitted to doing it, but everyone knew it was she, and she just smiled.

Her pranks would come on suddenly and hit you before you even knew it. I would think to myself, *If only I could think as well as her in this area and get her back and get her back good.* I felt I needed to take a class from her on the art of pranks and sarcasm. After all, she was the Christian education director; there had to be some way she could fit it in as a Sunday school class or something. The beauty of Kristy is that she loves the Lord with all her heart and will go out of her way to serve you and love you. So, being pranked by her almost seems like an honor because she never does it in a mean way.

One day it happened! My opportunity was right there in front of me. It was my turn to get her back for all of the tricks and scares she had brought my way over the years. Now, I know the Bible says to turn the other cheek, but in this case I really didn't think it would apply. It was almost like God Himself had placed the opportunity before me.

I need to set this whole thing up by saying, for several years Kristy suffered from asthma. Asthma so bad that there were a few times she almost died because she could not breathe. She was careful to limit her time doing strenuous work or work that would kick up a lot of dust and dirt.

This bright, sunny day, I happened to walk over to Kristy's house to visit and see what she was up to. She wasn't in the house, but I heard a noise from the backyard and realized she was out cleaning her camper after family church camp. As I approached the camper, I heard the sound of the vacuum coming from the back bedroom and saw it was plugged in right at the first step of the trailer. Just to be funny, I unplugged it and hid next to the trailer. I could hear her comment, "Hmm, okay." And then she came and plugged it back in. She just figured she must have pulled too hard, and it had come unplugged. Once she did that, she went back to work in the back of the trailer, bent all the way over to get the dirt in the corners.

I quietly sneaked into the trailer and walked as close to her as I could. When she stood up and turned around, she was standing extremely close to me, and I just screamed to scare the tar out of her. She threw the vacuum extension and screamed and screamed and screamed. I had accomplished my goal. I had scared my sister-in-law, was laughing hysterically, and was basking in my victory. However, as she walked out from behind the bed into the eating area, I realized her screams had turned to heavy breathing and gasping. Could it be true? Had I scared her so badly she had gone into an asthma attack? The answer? *Yes.* In the midst of her gasps for breath I heard the words, "That. Was. A. Good. One, Laurie."

She was dying but had given me the reward I needed. When Kristy Castle says a prank is good, you know it is because she is the best. Her mentorship in the art of pranking had paid off. The poor gal was still gasping for breath, and all I could do was laugh and laugh. I didn't think she was going to die, but she surely couldn't breathe very well. I figured she'd let me know if it was awfully serious or if I needed to take her to the hospital. But for the moment, I would just enjoy my moment as the Queen of Prank.

After sitting together at the table for a few minutes, her asthma attack finally calmed down, and she was back to normal. I hadn't killed the pastor's wife. (That would have been a downer to try to explain to my husband.) Thankfully, because it wouldn't have looked so good in the small-town paper, especially since she was my sister-in-law too. Can you imagine the headline? "Sister-in-law *kills* well-known pastor's wife in silly prank!" I did have to count the cost for this one because I knew that with it, at some point, it was going to come back around to me again. So, I moved to Mexico!

Digging Deeper

1. It's nice to have a good friend. We need people around us with whom to spend time laughing and doing silly things. Think of some fun, silly, unusual things you have done with or to a friend.

2. In the Bible two of the most well-known best friends were David and Jonathan. These two were as close as brothers. Here is a glimpse of their friendship in 1 Samuel 20:4 (NIV). "Jonathan said to David, 'Whatever you want me to do, I'll do for you.'" Wow! Do you have a friend you would say that to?

3. Are there things you need to do to be a better friend? What sacrifices can you make this week for a good friend?

Chapter 22

7-11's Flying Cups

Sitting in our nearly empty house in Mexico, I watched the movers pack up our things. I knew I was soon going to have to give them my beloved coffee pot to be put away in a box until it arrived in Michigan. It was early morning when they pried it from my hands to live in its new home, *the box*. It was then I knew my afternoon coffee would have to be found elsewhere. Those who know me are fully aware I am a coffee snob. I mean, come on, after living in Costa Rica for eight months near several coffee plantations and the freshest coffee ever, how could I not be?

The movers were making advances in the packing by late afternoon, and I needed (okay, that's a little dramatic) a cup of coffee. I knew it wouldn't be *my* coffee, but the 7-11 in our neighborhood usually brewed a semi-satisfying pot. I drove up there and realized the already-made coffee had been sitting on their burner for forty-five minutes. Yuck! I just couldn't do it. I imagined a slightly strong and burnt taste. I smiled at the worker and, in my best Spanish (rusty after ten months of non-use), said, "What are the chances you could brew me a new pot?"

He replied that they change it every hour and that there was still fifteen minutes to wait. Being the American I am, waiting is not in my blood. I must have looked like a sad puppy because he stood there and thought a moment. Without a word, he began making a new, fresh pot of coffee. I was elated. Oh, I could wait five minutes, knowing that I would get the desired caffeinated goodness. So wait I did, with much joy and anticipation.

He had been very kind to fulfill my request, probably at the risk of getting in trouble for making the coffee too soon. I'm sure he'd tell his boss something like, "Look, this big, tall *gringa* lady kept muttering something about needing fresh coffee, and she just kept staring at me. Seriously, this was the only way to get her out of our store quickly, señor."

And with that, the boss would understandingly reply, "Yes, she was in last night, trying to speak Spanish. I didn't have a clue what she said, so I just smiled. When she left, I rolled my eyes, hoping she'd never return. I was wrong; she came today to you, son. You passed the gringa test—you are now manager. *Felicidades!*" I'm sure this is not what really happened, but I'm certain there had to have been some sort of conversation.

Once the coffee was made, I stood where the different-sized cups were fitted into their appropriate areas under the counter. There was one sleeve of large cups on either side of me. When I went to take out one cup, about six popped out of their spring, and I knew that if I didn't push them in someone would walk by and catch a leg on them.

As any responsible person would do, I proceeded to push them back into place, where the spring would catch them. When they wouldn't budge, I pushed harder and then saw the *button*. *Ah, yes*, I said to myself—the button. I pushed it. What happened next surprised me to no end. When I pushed it, *all* of the cups shot out onto the floor. Really? Shooting cups? So I picked them up and put them on the counter. I then reached with my left hand to the sleeve of cups on my left side, which also sat in its little spring holder. I knew better than to push any buttons. I had learned my lesson. Again, five or six sprang out, and I just gently pushed the rest back in. Suddenly, the spring let loose and again. Yes, again, ten-to-fifteen cups shot out to the floor. At this point, I was just amazed. I looked at the same guy, who was now at the counter with a customer, and I said in Spanish, "Is this a joke?"

I honestly thought there was going to be something like *Candid Camera* there. He just looked at me strangely (as I find most people do when I'm in a store in Latin America) as I picked up the cups and flipped them over onto the counter. I quickly picked two cups from the middle, filled them, paid, and left.

On our last full day in Mexico, I couldn't even go to the store and get two simple cups of coffee. I'll certainly be glad to get my own coffee pot back, my special blend of beans, my liquid *foo-foo* fancy creamer, and my ceramic cups that don't shoot out of the cupboards at me.

Digging Deeper

1. What type of impression do you leave with people? When people talk about you, what are the characteristics they list?

2. Second Corinthians 2:15 (NIV) says, "We are to God the pleasing aroma of Christ among those who are being saved and those who are perishing."

3. Think about the fragrance you leave behind to others when you are at your job, at school, at the grocery store, etc. Is it an aroma others would like to have around them? Or are you like me in the 7-11, where the guy just couldn't wait to get me out of there?

The Many Faces
of Laurie

Part II

Lost in Translation and Other Short Ditties

Chapter 23

The Americans Grace the Grocery Stores

For some reason I like to go grocery shopping. Many of my friends think I am odd for liking this activity, but I just like to go and look at things casually at my own pace and without pressure. Living for a time in small-town Michigan, I liked being able to go to the local grocery store and run into people I knew. Chitchatting for a bit in the coffee aisle or at the register is just something I love.

Living now in a city of a million people in Mexico, I go to the store and don't know anyone. It's strange for me, but I always try to smile at people and be nice as I walk the aisles, knowing they may need some encouragement for the day. Some days, however, it is probably good that I don't know anyone in the stores here, or I would be terribly embarrassed.

Sometimes I wonder if going to the store is worth it. Will something embarrassing happen each time our family walks into a Mexican store? Are we destined to stick out even more by doing something exceptionally dumb on each visit? I've come to realize that it doesn't happen every time. There are days my family and I can walk in, get what we want, and walk out without incident. Maybe those other days are to keep us humble and to help us realize we need God's help in every situation—even grocery shopping.

No, Thank You

One hot Saturday in Mexico, I spent the day at home but soon realized I needed to go to the grocery store. My son Zach and I began our journey together to eventually end up at the grocery store. First, our weekly trip to get the five-gallon jugs filled with purified water, then to grab a movie, and then to Super Del Norte (the store closest to our house) to buy a few groceries. We finally ended up at the grocery store to get our things and proceeded to the check-out line. The stores in Mexico always have young kids packing the groceries for customers, who tip them about twenty or thirty cents. When the twelve-year-old boy had finished packing our bags, he asked me a question, to which I replied, *"No, gracias."*

I was pretty confident he asked if I needed help out to my car with the groceries, and I replied politely. As we took a few more steps away from him, Zach told me what he had really said to me. He had said, "Happy Children's Day," to which I replied, "No, thanks."

Could I really be that mean? That poor little boy, having an American lady burst his bubble of a wonderful Children's Day. From that day forward, he probably thought we Americans don't like kids. Well, if you think about it and look on our calendars, we have days for moms, dads, and grandparents, etc., but there isn't a day to celebrate kids.

When we returned home, my children asked me why, in the United States, didn't we have a day especially to celebrate children. My reply was simply, "Every day is kids' day!" No more was ever said about Children's Day again.

If at First You Don't Succeed Talk Louder?

Returning to the same store one day, we had to buy some more things. This time Mitchell went inside with me. He was looking for oatmeal. A young girl was mopping the floor in the aisle where Mitch thought the oatmeal might be. Like most fourteen-year-old boys his age speaking to this girl for the first time, he spoke timidly and asked her in Spanish if they carried oatmeal. She gave him kind of a blank look. Because he thought she didn't understand him, he did what most Americans would do when speaking to someone in another language; he decided to ask louder. She pointed to her ear, as if telling him she couldn't hear him. As he was about to repeat the question even louder, he suddenly stopped himself and clued in that she was telling him she was deaf. *Oh! She can't hear me*, he thought. *Phew, it's not my poor Spanish. Even if I was speaking Japanese she couldn't hear me.* He was still embarrassed and couldn't get out of there fast enough. I'm not sure if we ever got the oatmeal. Guess we would have to eat cold cereal.

Buffers and Bakeries

If you know anything about the bakeries in Mexico, you know that to stop in for hot, freshly-made bread or pastries is an experience you won't want to miss. Zachary and I decided one day to make a side trip to a really good bakery. We pulled into the parking spot in front of the big picture window that went all the way to the ground. I was in awe of all of the fresh-baked goods we could see from the window, and my mouth was watering with delight because soon we would be going in and picking out anything we wanted.

What a joyous day of bakery goodness. Zach got out of the car, and I too started to get out, when the van lurched forward and hit what I thought was the window. Zachary was totally embarrassed; I think I was just in unbelief that the van had hit the big picture window. The van stopped. It was like slow motion as I waited for the window to shatter right there in front of me, all over the precious baked goods.

Nothing happened. I realized, in my bakery excitement, I had forgotten to put the van in park. I got out and slowly walked to the front of the van, wondering why it hadn't gone right through the store window. It was then I noticed that at bumper level there was a 4x4 long piece of cement across the window to protect it. (They must have known I was coming when they built it.) I had hit the cement buffer and not the glass. I was so thankful. Zachary was very glad because the donut he wanted would have been sprinkled with glass from Mom's van—not with the colorful sprinkles he had come to love.

We proceeded into the store and acted as if nothing happened, bought our baked goods, and left. I always wonder what people say about us when we leave a store. I bet it gives them good conversations and laughs for the rest of the day.

Lactose Intolerant

On one of my shopping days I thought it would be fun to invite my husband along. You see, he thinks more along the line of fun foods to buy for the family, and me, I just think of the practical necessities. Upon his suggestion we bought a coconut we could cut, drink the milk from, and then eat the meat. We also bought a bottle of ginger ale (something not very common here in Mexico) for the kids to split at dinner. Of course, the purchases I made were boring in comparison, such as dish soap, honey, lettuce, and eggs. But it was a neat perspective to browse with my husband. He showed me several fun things in the dairy section, which I usually just breeze right across.

It was in the dairy section that my troubles began. I was on one side of the aisle and he on the other. When he called me over to look at something, I quickly whipped the cart around to go toward him. And then it happened! One of the workers had come out of nowhere, and the second I turned the cart (with a lot of force and speed, I have to admit) was the second she walked by. I hit her so hard in the back of the leg with the cart she actually squealed. Limping followed that, which was followed by the stunned look on my face. All I could say was, "I'm sorry" in English, but I was in a

Spanish-speaking country, so I quickly had to change to Spanish.

"Lo siento mucho ... mucho ... mucho." I couldn't believe what she said to me. She said, "Don't worry." Now it's kind of hard not to worry when she is close to crying as she walks to meet her coworkers. I stopped what I was doing, and with all of the compassion I could muster went to her again and said how very sorry I was. As she was still clutching her leg, her friend turned to me and said, "Don't worry."

It was then I realized that, hmm, it must what they tell them to say in training if they ever get hit near the Achilles tendon with a cart by a giant American lady. I don't know, but they both had said it. My question was how could the friend tell me not to worry when she didn't even know how the girl was really feeling? It must have been the *go to* phrase in Mexico for such an incident as this. I'm wondering if, as an American, I would have used the same phrase. I'm not sure I would have been so nice, as I probably would have clutched my leg, fallen to the ground, and wailed like a baby.

I took the "don't worry" as truly a suggestion of what to do. We continued on with our shopping. I did finally see what Brian was trying to show me but, for the life of me, can't remember now what it was. Why? Because I was still worried. How could I just *not worry* when I had hurt this girl? I worried all the way through the store and am still worried tonight if I really did hurt her and made her bleed. I wonder if there is workman's compensation for that kind of accident. I think the next time I have to shop there I am going to avoid the dairy section all together. I think I've become lactose intolerant.

The Christmas Mocking

I really don't like to make people feel bad by the things I say. It's not that I am all that tender-hearted or that I'm all that nice, but I feel like the world is mean enough without me adding to it. Now I haven't always been this way, and that fact right there makes me sad. I remember being sent to the principal's office once in fourth grade for saying something really hurtful to someone. I don't know why I did it; it just seemed fun at the time.

I realize we are all human and that we will, at times, make people feel bad by our tone of voice or body language or a misunderstanding of communication, but to deliberately move forward to hurt someone just isn't my style. Or at least my goal is not to do it on purpose.

One day, Emily and I were in a little shop in our Mexican city, looking for some wrapping paper for a gift we were giving at a party that night. Three ladies were working at the counter, and no one else was there to be waited on, so all of the attention was on the two Americans. It was a gift for a going-away party, so I was trying to explain I didn't want Christmas wrapping or birthday wrapping; I wanted another kind of wrapping. So I asked the lady what the Spanish word was for this type of event. The one lady thought for a minute and said, "This type of event is called a *poshada*."

Well, that seemed easy enough for me to remember because another word for parties was *posada*. They seemed very close to the same sound. One with just an "s" and the one she told me with the "sh." Perfect. So I said to her, "So I know that a posada is like a Christmas party, and so a poshada must be this type of party? Interesting."

We spent a few more minutes there, and all three ladies helped me find just what I needed. They talked among themselves as I was elsewhere picking out a card for the gift I would wrap. As they were talking to each other, I noticed the lady who had explained my word to me had a speech impediment. I was beginning to realize what I had done and not even realized it.

I'm always eager to learn new words in Spanish, and when I hear one I like to repeat it, talk about it, and repeat it again to that person. I want it embedded in my brain. And that is just what I did with this nice lady. Except the difference here was that we were both saying the same word—posada. But with her speech impediment, it came out as poshada.

I quickly paid for my gift wrapping and walked with my dear, sweet little girl into the store next to that one. Emily just had to point out what I had done because I was, literally, dying on the inside. I had made fun of that lady and didn't even realize it. Emily sweetly said, "Mom, you could go back and apologize to her and tell her that you don't know Spanish very well and thought it was a new word."

I actually thought it might be a great idea; I then realized what usually happens in my life when I try to go back and *fix* things. I figured I would dig myself in deeper if I tried to say sorry.

We continued on with our day and our shopping venture. We were thankful when we had to walk back by their store and saw it was full of people, enough to where they probably didn't even notice us passing by. I prayed that afternoon the lady would not feel bad over what I had said. I always remember hearing as a kid, "Sticks and stones will break your bones, but words can never hurt you." I wondered if my words had hurt her that day.

Chapter 24

Reasons I Stick to Women's Ministries

My passion in ministry has always been working with women. I feel comfortable talking to women, and obviously, because I am a woman, I can *get* where they are coming from. I have to work a bit more when it comes to talking with men, knowing what to say to them, and especially, in a different culture, figuring out what's appropriate and what's not.

Yuck! I Kissed a Sweaty Man

In Mexico men greet each other differently than women do. Women shake right hands and pull each other in for an *air* kiss on the right cheek—very simple—and you catch on quickly. Men, however, turn their heads in the opposite direction than the women, give a big hug, pat each other's backs, and then shake hands. It's customary here in Mexico to greet everyone individually and do the air kisses, hugs, etc.

One day, a man, whom I had never met, greeted me. Because I didn't know the *guy* protocol, I went to give him the lady's greeting of the air kiss on the cheek. He chose to greet me like he would greet a man. I saw it coming but couldn't stop myself fast enough before I had kissed the man's neck! Oh, it wasn't an air kiss on the neck; it was a true, I-just-kissed-you-on-the-neck kiss. It was sweaty. I was shocked at what had just happened. And I'm not going to lie, I was completely grossed-out. I wanted to die of embarrassment!

Working with women, I automatically know what kind of greeting to expect, and I don't have to worry about things like that. The worst that might happen when greeting a woman is that her lipstick may leave a smudge on my cheek. I think I will surely take that over kissing a stranger's sweaty neck.

Dirty Man

We had started attending a church here in Mexico and were getting to know people there and enjoying the comradery. Most people in this country have their given names, but many have nicknames. Because it is less formal, we try as hard as we can to remember those nicknames. We have a friend named Jesús, but everyone calls him *Suso*, an easy name to remember unless you are trying to remember everyone else's nicknames as well in another language.

After several Sundays of calling him Jesús, I made a decision that this particular Sunday I was going to greet him by using his nickname, Suso. I remember riding in the car on the way to church, practicing in my mind how I was going to greet him by using his nickname. *"Hola, Suso, como estas?"*

(Hi, Suso, how are you doing?) How could I mess that up? I find it funny now that I had to psych myself up to just call him by his nickname, but I did.

I entered the church with my kids behind me, and there he was, right inside the door. I extended my hand and with all of the joy I could muster said, *"Hola, Susio, como estas?"*

My kids, who had looks of sheer embarrassment on their faces, said, "Oh, Mom!" and did a quick about-face away from me. What had I done? I replayed the scene quickly in my head. Oh, my! I had said "Hello, Susio." Susio in Spanish means dirty. I had said "Hello, dirty man." Yikes! One letter made the difference, and I had messed this one up good. Fortunately, he laughed and corrected me by saying, "It's Suso." And we went on with our Sunday service. Suso, his wife, and I still laugh about that day because six years later, we are good friends with them.

Never Ask a Man that Question

I am a relational person; I always like to try to make people feel comfortable. Obviously, with Suso and my kids, they felt very uncomfortable. But for the most part, I like to seek people out who aren't being engaged in conversation and visit with them.

When we first moved to Mexico, we had been going to a Bible study at a friend's home. Every week was a learning experience for us as we tried to listen to the fast talking in Spanish and attempt to read aloud from the Bible when called upon to do so.

One particular week, the new pastor came and visited the study. Afterward, most of the group was getting food ready in the other room. I was left at the table with the new pastor, while my husband (also at the table) was kind of half-listening while doing something else. Because I wanted to make the pastor feel welcome, I began to try to speak to him in my best Spanish (which, at that time, was not very good).

My intention was to ask him if he had been able to visit with many people during the previous week he had been there. He gave me a strange look (which is never a good sign), and my husband just shook his head. For during his half-listening, he had heard what I'd asked the new pastor. The pastor very kindly said to me in good English, "Yes, what I think you are asking is if I have visited with many people this week, and I have. What you really asked me was if I had assassinated many people this week, and I haven't."

I had just asked the new pastor if he had assassinated anyone that week. Are you kidding me? Still, Brian just shook his head at the wonder of how I could even come up with these words. As I looked back on the conversation, the even scarier part about that question was we were living right on the border of Mexico, where a lot of drug violence and killings were taking place. Asking people in that city if they had assassinated anyone that week might result in a yes answer. Thankfully, the pastor had mercy, hadn't killed anyone that week, and had understood enough English to tell me of my error.

Chapter 25

Money Really Is the Root of All Evil ... or at Least Most of My Mishaps

I've never been used to having a lot of money, so I am used to thinking in small numbers. I've never been good at math, so the thought of having to add prices and figure out tips at restaurant is something I always refer to my husband and my kids. I just don't want to bother with it. Having lived in other countries, the money thing really throws me off. So I have to be very careful that I truly know what I am spending.

Several years ago in Mexico City, I paid over two dollars for a Snickers bar and had no idea I'd done so until my husband told me later. Our rent in Costa Rica was $1,300,000.00 colonies ($650 USD), so the idea of being a millionaire was pretty exciting for me until I realized I was going to have to keep track of all of those numbers. Then I had real fear—much fear.

Just let me think in small numbers and American dollars, and I do pretty well. After being in the United States for a year of home assignment, we had just returned to Mexico. I had to start thinking, not in American dollars, but in pesos. One would think that after living in Mexico before for five years, it wouldn't be that hard. But I'm finding my mind is a little slow in this area. The sad thing is that the evidence of this comes through when I am in public, and other people have to see it. It becomes a daunting experience for me, which makes me want to flee back to the United States, where the money is *normal*. Well, normal for me and what I am accustomed to.

Yes, Little Girl, I Am an Intelligent Woman

Emily and I had to stop at a *papeleria* on our way home from school one day. A papeleria is a small, privately-owned store that sells school supplies. These types of stores are all over the city.

This particular day, I decided to go to the one closest to our house, since we would probably be going there often. Emily needed a protractor, a piece of poster board, and a notebook. The lady behind the counter proceeded to help us, as well as helping a man and his daughter. The man spoke English, so he was able to help us figure out the word for protractor in Spanish (a word I don't find myself using every day).

The sales lady added it all up and pushed her calculator toward me to show me the price. I think she was being nice, knowing it would be easier for me (as an American) to see the price instead of trying to struggle to hear it. She was very right. She turned the calculator around so I could read the numbers, and it said twenty. I was in shock, to say the least! It was twenty dollars for those three little items? Are you kidding me? *No way!*

So I told Emily we could only get the poster board. I paid for the poster board, and we left the store. I explained to Emily that twenty dollars was way too much to spend for those items, and we would go to a different store where, hopefully, we could get things cheaper. As we stood there for a second, I looked at the receipt, and then it hit me. It hit me hard! It wasn't twenty dollars; it was twenty pesos, which is about $1.55. Oh, no.

So I did what any good mother would do and returned to the store to tell the lady I had made a mistake by thinking in American dollars. She chuckled, and the man who spoke English said it was understandable. By then, there was a little girl and her mom in the store, and the mom just smiled. We bought the other two things and left the store.

As we were walking out, the other mother and her daughter walked out at the same time. This is when Emily heard from the little girl, "Mom, what was her deal? She couldn't even figure out what twenty pesos is?"

Mothers universally have a way of having each other's backs. She stuck up for me. She told her daughter that we were from the United States, and sometimes the changing of money is hard. Bless that dear, sweet lady. Of course, her daughter still thought I was a dullard and probably the lady who sold me the items did as well. The true joy for me was that another mom stuck up for me. And as we got into the car, lovely Emily told me it would be okay.

Now, when we go to that store, I make her go in without me, just until they have time to forget me. Do you think they will ever forget me there? That was only two weeks into our stay here, so I'm sure things were bound to get better.

Eating Humble Pie ... Again

Just a few weeks after our protractor shopping at the papeleria, the whole money thing happened again. This time it was even more humiliating and embarrassing. I stopped to get gas on the way home and, of course, stopped at the gas station closest to the house. I had a $500 bill in my hand (which, in pesos, is the equivalent of about forty American dollars, and the word in Spanish is *quinientos*).

I flashed the $500 and asked the guy to put in *cinquenta*. Normally the $500 almost fills the tank, and I have to wait a few minutes. It was filled in about two minutes, and he asked for the money. There was no way the tank could have been filled that quickly. Thus I surmised he was ripping me off! It wouldn't fill up that fast. I started my car to see how far the gauge went, and it didn't even get to the tank's halfway mark.

I was not pleased. I confidently told him, in Spanish, I wouldn't pay him but wanted to speak with his manager. He showed me the numbers on the pump, and all I saw was the number five. I was just focused on talking to his manager. I would tell him how I had asked for $500 to be put into the tank, and his employee had only put in this small amount while ready to collect my $500, probably trying to rip me off because I'm an American and didn't know any better.

Interrupting my thoughts of what I planned to say to his manager, the young man, in a bit of confusion and dismay, shrugged his shoulders and pointed me toward the office. I pulled my car around, got out with my receipt in hand, and was ready to do some talking. I looked at the receipt to make sure I had all of my ducks in a row.

Then I saw it. *Oh, no. Not again!* I was wrong. I had asked him to put in cinquenta, which is fifty pesos or the American equivalent of four dollars. No wonder it hardly took any time at all. I was so utterly embarrassed as I peeked around and saw the attendant there waiting for me to go into the office to talk to his boss. There was nothing else I could do, so I had to swallow my pride and say to the attendant, "Look, I made a huge mistake. I was wrong, and you were right. Would you please forgive me?"

I then drove away, with hardly any gas in my tank at all, but thankful that the little bit would at least get me out of there. Would this ever end? Would I ever be able to actually look at a peso and not think of it in American dollars? Only time would tell, but until then, I think I better do my business in places that aren't so close to my house.

Chapter 26

From the Mouths of Babes

There are times when we say the wrong word at the wrong time and die a thousand deaths of embarrassment, hoping the conversation will end soon. We all have had those times. I recall seeing a lady from our church I hadn't seen in years. She happened to have been really heavy when I knew her before. When I saw her again years later, I couldn't believe my eyes. She looked wonderful. I proceeded to say, "Wow, you've lost tons!" In my mind, I was giving her the highest of compliments, but I wonder what went through hers as I chose the word *tons*?

I want to teach my children when it's appropriate to say certain things and when it's not. But when Mom struggles and doesn't even realize it until afterward, then it's kind of hard to give them a playbook on the art of keeping one's mouth closed.

Praying He Won't Notice

When my son Mitchell was about two-and-a-half years old, we took him into Target after the Christmas season.

We had to return something to the service counter, so we waited our turn in line until a nice young man called us to his station. This man must have had problems with his vision, which glasses could not completely correct because attached to his glasses was a thing that almost looked like a jeweler's magnifying glass. When he read our receipt, he had to hold it very close to this device.

To try to give our arms a break, we sat Mitchell up on the counter, which was about chest high to us. He proceeded to study the man who read our receipt and said in a very loud voice, "Hee-hee. Look at that silly little man."

You can imagine the embarrassment coursing through my whole body at that moment. What could I say? What could I do? Should I run away and let Brian deal with this most embarrassing child? It was then my wise husband told Mitchell (in front of this man) it was important for him to have the device on his glasses so that he could see better to help us with what we needed.

Now that was everything my son needed to hear to move on with his life. But me, I couldn't wait to get out of there. I wondered if the man felt badly when he thought about the incident during his day or if he was callous to the comments people might make on a daily basis. Thankfully, Mitchell, now a grown man, has seen throughout his life many people and their handicaps and loves them for who they are inside.

Kisses of God

My middle son, Zachary, was about three years old when we were working in the church kitchen with some other people on an event taking place that day. A lady attended the church who was a kind, loving, and wonderful person. She just so happened to have moles all over her face. This was not a big deal because we knew her, loved her, and had spent quite a bit of time with her. Her friends didn't even see them anymore—they saw her. However, when Zach saw her for the first time, he looked up with all of the innocence of a child and asked, "What's that stuff all over her face?"

I know he was only three years old, but I stood there trying to figure out what to say, knowing that the comment had to have hurt her. The normally quick-thinking mother I am was, at that moment, standing dumbfounded, coming up with nothing to ease the awkwardness. Thankfully, one of the other dear ladies (and a very good friend to this woman) said to Zachary, "Those? Why those are the extra special kisses that God gave her for us all to see."

I was amazed at the wisdom of this woman and how she so gently answered Zach. He was satisfied with her response, went on with his day, and never mentioned it again.

Stopped in Her Tracks

Emily was about three years old when we went Christmas caroling at a nursing home. (Notice the ages of my kids when they said these things. They were just starting to talk, and

151

process experiences. If they had something on their minds, they would say it.) At one point, we were supposed to go and greet the residents and encourage them in a personal way. Emily walked beside us, and heads turned as they saw this beautiful little girl with long, flowing, curly hair. We actually walked a little bit past a man when she stopped, turned around, and with a quizzical look on her face, said, "Hmm, one leg. Would ya look at that?"

Sure enough, there was a man in a wheelchair in the hallway with one leg. As a parent, you really have to think quickly at such times. And because I never want to hurt anyone's feelings or have a family member do so, I just wanted to ease the situation quickly. We stopped and talked for a while with the man, and Emily was never bothered by the fact that he had only one leg. She just talked and talked with him. An embarrassing moment turned into a nice, encouraging visit for this man and for us.

The Big Question

One day, after a particularly embarrassing comment that I had made, Emily asked me a question. "Did your mom have the same struggles with saying and doing embarrassing things like you do?"

Now most moms could easily have been offended, but I totally understood her question. At ten years of age, she's a pretty smart cookie, and she is beginning to see the pattern of my life. Things happen to Mom; they just do. She understands that much of it I bring on myself, but some of the things just come out of nowhere and happen. It's an understood thing in our family—we talk about it, we laugh about it, and my children try not to follow in my footsteps in that area.

What it came down to was the fear of a little girl who was trying to answer the questions so prevalent in her mind. *Would I end up like Mom? Was I going to grow up and do the same thing? Is this hereditary?* She told me she sometimes found herself doing the same things, and it made her wonder. Poor, sweet girl—Mamma's girl! I didn't have the heart to tell her it only gets worse with age. I think she'll figure it out. For that, I must tell her at an early age, "I'm sorry." Maybe in twenty years, you'll be reading a book of *her* stories.

Notes

1   Crockpot. *Crockpot, the Original Slowcooker, Classic, for use with 4-7 quart manual slow cookers, Owner's Guide*, June 13, 2008, accessed June 26, 2015, http://demandware.edgesuite.net/ aamb_prd/on/demandware.static/Sites-crock-pot-Site/Sites-crock-pot-Library/default/dwfff64052/documents/instruction-manuals/SCR500-SS_43_68388868.PDF, 3.

2   William Shakespeare, *All's Well that Ends Well* in *Mr. William Shakespeare's Comedies, Histories, & Tragedies or The First Folio* (London: Edward Blount and Isaac Jaggard Publishers, 1623), Act One, Scene One.

3   Noah Webster, *American Dictionary of the English Language* (New York: S. Converse Publisher, 1828), Volume 1, 102.

Made in the USA
Lexington, KY
03 November 2015